D0920086

THE
INFORMATION
SOCIETY

THE
INFORMATION
SOCIETY

a sceptical view

christopher may

polity

RARITAN VALLEY COMMUNITY COLLEGE
EVELYN S. FIELD LIBRARY

Copyright © Christopher May 2002

The right of Christopher May to be identified as author of this work has been asserted in accordance with the Copyright, Designs and Patents Act 1988.

First published in 2002 by Polity Press in association with Blackwell Publishers Ltd

Editorial office:
Polity Press
65 Bridge Street
Cambridge CB2 1UR, UK

Marketing and production:
Blackwell Publishers Ltd
108 Cowley Road
Oxford OX4 1JF, UK

Published in the USA by
Blackwell Publishers Inc.
350 Main Street
Malden, MA 02148, USA

All rights reserved. Except for the quotation of short passages for the purposes of criticism and review, no part of this publication may be reproduced, stored in a retrieval system, or transmitted, in any form or by any means, electronic, mechanical, photocopying, recording or otherwise, without the prior permission of the publisher.

Except in the United States of America, this book is sold subject to the condition that it shall not, by way of trade or otherwise, be lent, re-sold, hired out, or otherwise circulated without the publisher's prior consent in any form of binding or cover other than that in which it is published and without a similar condition including this condition being imposed on the subsequent purchaser.

ISBN 0-7456-2684-X
ISBN 0-7456-2685-8 (pbk)

A catalogue record for this book is available from the British Library and has been applied for from the Library of Congress.

Typeset in 10½ on 12 pt Palatino
by SNP Best-set Typesetter Ltd., Hong Kong
Printed in Great Britain by TJ International, Padstow, Cornwall.

This book is printed on acid-free paper.

Contents

Preface

While writing this book the much trumpeted 'new economy' came a little unstuck, leading one stock market commentator to proclaim in the headline to their column: 'Fact: the new economy does not exist' (Motley Fool 2001). In a less extreme form of this disillusionment, a *Financial Times* editorial concluded: 'The information economy is real, if neither as revolutionary nor as profitable as some hoped. The economy is not new, but it is not simply old, either' (Financial Times 2001). To some extent I have been amused by the bursting of the dotcom bubble, but despite some *schadenfreude*, I also know that many people, who did not deserve to, lost money (pensions and savings) because they believed what the technology analysts told them at the beginning of 2000. This is a useful example of the dangers of accepting the 'fact' of the information age. As I listened to stock market advice proffered over the table at lunch in the staff common room at my university, while the bubble lasted, I was reminded of a story about the stock market crash in 1929. The Rockefellers pulled all of their money out of stocks and shares a few days before the crash. When asked how he had been so prescient, John Rockefeller replied that he knew the market had peaked when bus-boys operating the lifts at the Waldorf Astoria gave him stock tips. In the spring and summer of 2000, talking to colleagues, who were also picking stocks (though thankfully not actually investing any money), I thought to myself 'there's a crash coming.'

As many commentators have now been forced to accept, the information society and its 'new economy' have not invalidated previous ideas about economics. And, as I note in the final chapter, worries about the price of oil have resurfaced. If the economy was truly 'weightless' as some commentators have suggested, then the price of oil would have little real impact. As it is, governments and economists in the most developed countries have started to warn that a prolonged period of higher than trend oil prices will likely lead to major economic problems, a slowdown in economic growth and possibly recession. It seems the old ideas we had about economics are not quite as invalid as the information society celebrants would have us believe. This is reinforced by an excellent Marxian critique of lean production and the 'new economy' (Smith 2000) which I came across as I was finishing my final draft. Although Tony Smith develops a more detailed argument than I do in chapter 3, he reaches similar conclusions, and for those interested in the issues I raise there (and in chapter 2's discussion regarding the 'logic' of capital), Smith's book is useful further reading.

In the following chapters, as above, I sometimes refer to the 'information economy'. I use this term to highlight the specific sectors of the 'information society' which are clearly and directly linked to the economy. Although these terms are frequently used interchangeably both in the media and by other commentators, I have endeavoured to differentiate between them in use, as the information society is not *only* the information economy, despite the latter being the main focus of many treatments of the 'information age'. Additionally I want to stress that there is much useful (and positive) work starting to appear which identifies examples of newly emerging political networks and virtual communities outside the core information societies, linking diasporas together and providing new possibilities for political engagement. While these developments may expand and come to change the politics of the information society, currently their full impact remains in the future (with the exceptions I discuss in chapters 4 and 5). While I do not mean to dismiss important political movements, too many other accounts of the information age have fastened on to such minority developments to give a positive spin to the contemporary information society. Given the sceptical intent of this book, I have left the celebration of these new networks and communities to others.

Finally, if there is one thing that I would want you to take away from this book, it is that our ideas about society which have taken so long to develop and refine are not immediately invalidated by the information society. It is not the end of history, it is not the dawning of a new age. If you already believe there is a great deal of continuity with the past, then I hope this book will give you some useful ammunition to utilize when you are up against those who proclaim all is new. If you are not so sure, then I hope this book will convince you of my argument, or at least prompt you to consider it.

Acknowledgements

This book reflects an expansion of an interest related to my previous work on intellectual property rights, and grew out of a course I taught at the University of the West of England (Bristol): 'Global Information Society? From LA to Frenchay'. I have gained valuable insights from the students I have discussed these issues with and have enjoyed explaining (and defending) my position to an often sceptical audience. I would especially like to thank the following students who offered particularly helpful comments during seminars and other discussions the first year the course was run: Natalie Addo, Jennifer Britton, Natasha Brown, Natalie Carter, Daniel Crouch, Patrick Delany, Catherine Dodkin, Pauline Grant, Jennifer Harries, Juliet Hart, Rebecca Hartly, Steve Hunt, Chris Hutchings, Nicola Kinloch, Vicky May, Nicholas Moore, Stephen Moore, Susanah Nowlan, Marion Reiser and Rupert Wertheimer. This book is partly intended to fill a gap in the contemporary literature which revealed itself when I looked for books to recommend to them.

During the writing of this book, and of the articles which explored specific issues covered by the various chapters, a number of colleagues and friends have read and commented on various drafts. I want to especially thank Andrew Chadwick who has read virtually everything included here and helped me improve its style and content. I am also grateful for the help and support of Richard Barbrook, Robin Brown, Edward Comor, Claire Cutler, Marianne Franklin, Ursula Huws, Douglas Kellner, Brian Loader, David Mason, Jonathan Nitzan, Jayne Rodgers, Susan Sell, Tim Sinclair, Neil Spencer and Grahame Thompson, all of whom have commented on papers where I have explored the issues I discuss in this book. Two referees also offered useful comments which helped improve the final text. However, any shortcomings remain my responsibility alone.

I also want to thank all the members of the British International Studies Association, International Communications Working Group, who have provided me with a forum in which to discuss the issues developed in this book on many occasions. The workshops are always interesting, helpful and a friendly space to try out ideas. (Information on the group can be obtained from Jayne Rodgers, jayne@ics-server.novell.leeds.ac.uk)

My family has as always been very supportive. My mother, Laurie May (very much *old* Labour), read the whole manuscript as a representative of the lay reader, and those outside the academy who read this book will have benefited from her questions regarding the details of the arguments. Hilary (my wife) continues to wonder what exactly I am doing in my study but is unceasing in her support for my work. Without her this book would never have been finished. My late father, still a major intellectual influence, introduced me to the work of Lewis Mumford, and this book would not have been the same had I not been his son. Finally I would also like to thank John Thompson, Gill Motley and the staff of Polity for their invaluable support and immediate enthusiasm for this project. And, during production, Ann Bone's excellent copy-editing has improved the text and in many places helped clarify my meaning. Some aspects of the arguments presented in this book were first laid out in:

'The Information Society as Mega-Machine: The Continuing Relevance of Lewis Mumford', *Information Communication and Society*, vol. 3, no. 2 (Summer 2000), pp. 1–25.

'Information Society, Task Mobility and the End of Work', *Futures*, vol. 32, no. 5 (May 2000), pp. 399–416.

'Capital, Knowledge and Ownership: The Information Society and Intellectual Property', *Information, Communication and Society*, vol. 1, no. 3 (Autumn 1998), pp. 245–68.

My analysis of intellectual property was originally developed in:

A Global Political Economy of Intellectual Property Rights: The New Enclosures? Routledge/Review of International Political Economy Studies in Global Political Economy (London: Routledge, 2000).

The very forces of matter, in their blind advance, impose their own limits. That is why it is useless to want to reverse the advance of technology. The age of the spinning-wheel is over and the dream of a civilisation of artisans is in vain. The machine is only bad in the way that it is now employed. The benefits must be accepted even if its ravages are rejected.

Albert Camus, *The Rebel*

Again, for Hilary

and

for all the *Next*-besuited Philanthropists
of the information age*

---

* with apologies to Robert Tressell

1

What is the Global Information Society?

It will not have escaped your notice that there are many people who claim we have entered a new age, governed by a 'new paradigm' where society and its economic relations are no longer primarily organized on the basis of material goods. Rather, they claim, now everything is organized on the basis of information and knowledge, or soon will be. Often referred to as the arrival of a (global) information society, sometimes discussed as a 'weightless world' or a new network society, in the past this change has been characterized as the arrival of a postindustrial or service society. In this book I take some key elements of this contention and argue there is less to these changes than tales of transformation suggest. Simply put, while we may be living through a period in which the form and practices of our lives are changing in many ways, the underlying substance of our socioeconomic system remains largely the same.

We are often told that new information and communication technologies (ICTs), perhaps best represented by the internet, are changing everything: this is a revolution, a remaking of the world. All we previously knew about our societies is useless for thinking about this new world. But, despite claims that 'grand narratives' are obsolete, the vision of an information society itself often takes the character of an all-encompassing story about this new age. For many this prompts celebration of an approaching utopia, while for others the developments described indicate progression towards a dystopian world like that set out in *Bladerunner*. However, I am sceptical: despite the claims about revolution (repeated on television, in the papers we read and even among ourselves), our lives in many ways remain relatively unchanged.

Most of us still need to go to work, where there remains an important division between those who run the company and those who work for it, not least in terms of rewards. When we look at what allows some of us to become rich and the rest of us merely to get by on our pay or pensions, this still has something to do with who owns what. In discussions of the information society, significantly, one of the changes most often identified has been in the sorts of things which produce the greatest wealth. In the past it might have been (part) ownership of a company (through stocks and shares) or land and buildings; now it is as likely to be the rights to a particular artistic creation (films, songs, books) or the rights to an innovative technical process. This new property is called intellectual property, and although different from material property in many ways, it still leaves us divided between those who have some of significant value and those who have only a little or none. Thus, while all sorts of claims are made about the ways in which our lives are being transformed by new ICTs, many social patterns (especially how wealth is distributed) continue as before. When we strip away the shiny new products and services which are available to us in ever increasing quantities, much about the world has not changed.

This is a sceptical view of the information age. Of course it is not the only view, but it is one that makes more sense to me than the celebratory chorus I hear so often when these subjects come up in the media, on the internet or when I am talking with colleagues and students. Let me be clear: I am not arguing that nothing is changing, but rather that these changes are not as profound as they are often presented. Underlying these shifts I see many continuities and it is those I wish to emphasize. I want to explore these continuities because I do not accept that the hard-won knowledge of modern life developed in the past is now outmoded or useless. The assertion that we are entering a new age attempts to neuter or defuse social criticisms which are as salient now as they were in the last millennium. I do not intend to deal with every variant of the information revolution thesis nor every author who has written about it in the last forty years. This would be a mammoth task and subject to diminishing returns. What I aim to do is utilize those authors who have made significant statements, and perhaps more importantly, those whose work has been often cited or used in subsequent discussions of the information age.

In the rest of this chapter I briefly discuss the development of the idea of an information society, and conclude by introducing the four key claims that are frequently made about this new era and which I discuss in the rest of the book. These have been often restated in the past thirty years and they are:

- that we are experiencing a social revolution;
- that the organization of economic relations has been transformed;
- that political practices and the communities involved are changing;
- and that the state and its authority are in terminal decline.

These four claims are related to each other. The notion of a social revolution is linked to changes in the ways economic relations are organized. Changes in economic relations are often related to shifts in the political landscape, and these shifts are unlikely to leave the role of the state unaltered. My criticisms of these assertions therefore represent related elements of my underlying argument that while the forms of activity have changed their substance remains the same. I recognize that the world cannot be divided so easily and clearly into what is changing and what is not, and neither is there a clear and distinct division between form and substance. Nevertheless, although a simplification, the distinction between changes in form and substance sums up my position so well that I am loathe to avoid it completely.

The Idea of an Information Society

The idea of an information society started to appear in accounts of contemporary society in the early 1960s, and until the 1980s claims made about the information revolution were subject to extensive interrogation. However, in the most recent rush to identify the (imminent) arrival of the global information society, criticism has been much more muted. Early analyses of the information society, from Fritz Machlup's groundbreaking study in 1962 of *The Production and Distribution of Knowledge in the United States* to Marc Porat's work on *The Information Economy* in the mid-1970s, focused on the United States. Only after 1976 did studies start to appear which looked outside America (Poirier 1990: 247–9). And while in the early 1990s interest seemed to be on the wane, the emergence of the internet as an increasingly mass medium has prompted a major expansion of interest in the information society. Consequently, we can identify three periods of analysis:

1   from 1962 to the mid-1970s analyses concentrated exclusively on America;
2   from the late 1970s to the early 1990s, as ICTs were deployed extensively in the rich or developed states, analyses looked further afield;
3   and now, analyses focus on the potential and promise of the internet, leading to the current widespread interest in the global information society.

Unsurprisingly, as the new ICTs became more and more widespread so speculation about their social impact expanded.

Where the global implications of the information society were recognized earlier, this usually focused on the problem of new knowledge (ideas and technologies) flowing (or not) from the centre outwards to developing countries; knowledge exports rather than the more recent notion of a networked world (Porat 1978; Dizard 1982: 148ff.). Indeed in the early 1980s both the United Nations Educational, Scientific and Cultural Organization (MacBride et al. 1980) and the Club of Rome (Friedrichs and Schaff 1982) produced semi-critical reports on ICTs and global society. However, more recently a number of powerful international governmental organizations have started to emphasize the benefits of the (global) information society and its links to economic development. To take three examples, the emergence of the information society was the defining logic for the 1998–9 *World Development Report: Knowledge for Development* (World Bank 1999), a major report to the United Nations Commission on Science and Technology for Development, *Knowledge Societies: Information Technology for Sustainable Development* (Mansell and Wehn 1998) and policy statements by the Organization for Economic Co-operation and Development such as *Towards a Global Information Society* (OECD 1997).

Although analysis of the idea of an information society got underway in earnest in the 1960s, the recognition of the economic value of knowledge and/or information was hardly unprecedented. Frank Knight explicitly accounted for the importance of knowledge activities and the workers who performed such tasks in *Risk, Uncertainty and Profit* published in 1921 (Poirier 1990: 246). And in 1959 Edith Penrose made the managerial control and development of knowledge resources a central element in her *Theory of the*

Growth of the Firm (Penrose 1995). But the realization that knowledge or information might be valuable is, of course, much older. For centuries patents have been awarded to valuable ideas, copyrights have constructed exclusive rights to creative works and trademark protection has recognized the value to be gained from the exclusive use of a maker's mark (Sell and May 2001). But, until the last third of the twentieth century, information was regarded as one input or resource among many, while knowledge was frequently assumed to be uncontainable. With the posited emergence of the information age, information is now becoming the input on which entrepreneurs concentrate, while the importance accorded to the control of (and access to) knowledge increasingly means that it *must* be contained, halting its 'free' distribution. It is these developments that lead many to herald a new age.

'Information society' emerges as an analytical concept

The origins of the idea of the information society can be traced to the work of Fritz Machlup. He was the first to categorize knowledge and information tasks separately from 'normal' industrial and social activities. He identified five sectors (education; media of communication; information machines; information services; other information activities) which could be measured and assigned economic value. This categorization, and the statistical measurement it enabled, allowed Machlup to claim in *The Production and Distribution of Knowledge in the United States* that in 1958 around 29 per cent of America's gross national product came from these 'knowledge industries' (Webster 1995: 11). Once a benchmark figure had been set, it was possible to measure any expansion of these sectors, and this was the evidence on which subsequent claims regarding the emergence of the information society were founded.

Without Machlup's work, Peter Drucker could not have argued a few years later that in the postwar period 'the base of our economy shifted from manual to knowledge work, and the centre of gravity of our social expenditure from goods to knowledge' (1968: 287). Drucker devoted nearly half *The Age of Discontinuity* to a discussion of 'knowledge techniques' and 'the knowledge society', arguing that the 'impact of cheap, reliable, fast and universally available information will easily be as great as was the impact of electricity' (1968: 27). Using an idea that was later central to Daniel Bell's work, Drucker suggested that while progress in the past had been based on the acquisition of experience, now 'systematic, purposeful, organized information' was the resource that would be deployed to advance society (1968: 40). Machlup's work enabled, or even encouraged, such claims.

Expanding on this statistical work, in the mid-1970s, Marc Porat's *The Information Economy* (a widely quoted and influential nine-volume report for the US government) suggested there were two complementary information sectors: the primary and the secondary. In the primary sector, knowledge industries manipulated knowledge and information to produce new knowledge products and services. In the secondary sector, knowledge and information manipulation was one part of material production processes, information being utilized in the production and sale of material outputs and the provision of services. The report claimed that, when taken together, these sectors accounted for over half of all economic activity in America (an increase on Machlup's figure), leading Porat to conclude that the US was fast becoming an information society (Webster 1995: 11–15). With its vast array of statistical evidence and its widely disseminated conclusions, Porat's report became a key piece of evidence in arguments regarding the transformation of society.

Despite being concerned primarily with the analysis of economic activities, a clear link between technological development and its social impact was always implied in these analyses. This led Wilson Dizard to rework Porat's sectors by conceptualizing them as three stages in the shift towards an information society in America, rather than as previously existing industrial sectors. In the first stage, large corporations deployed and developed various information technologies to produce new technical products. In the second, these new 'tools' were taken up by information industries and services. Finally, in the 'third and most far-reaching stage', this use would become so generalized that new networks would appear and transform the flows of information throughout society (Dizard 1982: 7). It was in this third stage that the social impact of these new technologies would become clear. This notion of progress towards the information society through the widening deployment of ICTs continues to be influential to this day.

Implications of the information society

Around the same time as Porat was compiling his report, Daniel Bell recognized similar shifts in *The Coming of Post-Industrial Society*

(1974). But Bell also suggested three more dynamics: theoretical knowledge would become increasingly important (a change in the 'axial principle' of society); expectations about the future would foreground issues of technology, its control and potential for transforming existence; and new decision-making processes would appear (1974: 14). He argued that methods of organizing social activities (the manner in which decisions are reached) could be regarded as 'intellectual technologies' which spread by example; successful techniques are copied by other actors and groups. Furthermore, 'the major source of structural change in society . . . is the change in the character of knowledge', a change which substitutes 'a technical order for the natural order' (1974: 44–5). This new knowledge order would increasingly set the agenda from which problems were addressed, defining the acceptable and unacceptable through the reduction of all problems to technical issues.

In the information age the role of the expert or technocrat would be enhanced. Bell recognized that knowledge had always been necessary in the functioning of society, but what would be

> distinctive about the post-industrial society is the change in the character of knowledge itself. What has become decisive for the organisation of decisions and the direction of change is the centrality of *theoretical* knowledge – the primacy of theory over empiricism and the codification of knowledge into abstract systems of symbols that . . . can be used to illuminate many different and varied areas of experience. (Bell 1974: 21)

In postindustrial society the 'central person is the professional' providing the 'services and amenities – health, education, recreation, and the arts – which are now deemed desirable and possible for everyone' (Bell 1974: 127). Bell characterized postindustrial society as a new set of 'games between people', a realm of individualized social existence. Classes and groups would be sidelined by the individual as the possessor and user of knowledge, but guided by (enlightened) technocratic governors. This idea of the rise of the individualized knowledge-adept social actor is one of the most repeated elements of the information age, although it is now seldom traced back to Bell's work.

In another early analysis of the effects of this new age, Alvin Toffler suggested that the feeling of dislocation and uneasiness many experienced in the late 1960s was directly linked to 'future shock', an inability to keep up with the accelerating changes of the nascent information age (Toffler 1970). This was, he later argued, because the postindustrial, information society was 'not a straight line extension of industrial society but a radical shift of direction . . . a comprehensive transformation at least as revolutionary' as the industrial revolution (Toffler 1980: 366). It is this disjuncture with the past, this new way of organizing society (Toffler's canvas stretched from psychology, through social relations to international relations), which resonates throughout the literature of the information society. Despite, or because of, their more journalistic tone, for many Alvin Toffler and John Naisbitt – whose *Megatrends* (1984) also foregrounded ICT-driven change – were the writers who first brought these ideas to an audience far outside the cloistered world of academia.

Once these early analyses of the postindustrial, information society had appeared, more and more accounts of the new age and its effects began to materialize. Indeed, Anthony Smith has argued these early writings on postindustrialism have 'a Hegelian ring about them. Information technology was penetrated by the historic spirit . . . [and] the very act of formulating this idea of an information and communication society has exercised much of the transforming power, or at least has provided the political acceleration [towards it]' (1996: 72). This is to say, the arguments for the emergence of the information society have reinforced the dynamic they claim to observe by contributing to the reorganization of socioeconomic relations they merely purport to 'recognize'. Postindustrial analyses which claim the information society is emerging have themselves contributed to the appearance of this new socioeconomic 'reality'. By arguing that these changes are real and require a response, social and economic development has been pushed in a particular direction. The responses suggested (and enacted) have actually reinforced (or even underpinned) the developments which these analyses argue have already taken place. In an important sense, the 'information society' as a characterization of the new technological age we are entering is a self-fulfilling prophecy.

Communication and the information society

It is also frequently argued that changes in ICTs have transformed the way we perceive the world. This is a proposition made famous by Marshall McLuhan, who had an ear for a catchy phrase and popularized such terms as the 'global village', the 'age of information' and 'the medium is the message'. Taking a historical perspective on information revolution(s), McLuhan focused in the first instance on the typographical innovations of the fifteenth century. He argued that the assumption embedded within typographical reproduction (the separation of language and information into recombinable units), alongside the more generally recognized expansion in the distribution of knowledge, was revolutionary, changing everything printing came into contact with (McLuhan 1962). Using his analysis of the impact of 'print culture', McLuhan then turned his attention to the effects of contemporary technological changes, outlined in his most famous book *Understanding Media*, first published in 1965 (McLuhan 1994). Trying to understand McLuhan is not an easy task, but his discussion of the transformative potential of new communication technologies and practices remains influential, inasmuch as many of his ideas find their way into current discussions, albeit unacknowledged.

The division of media into hot (closed, unidirectional/transmitted, complete messages) and cool (open, multidirectional/interactive messages requiring engagement) which McLuhan deploys at some length in *Understanding Media* has been seized on by those wishing to stress the interactive implications of internet-mediated information networks. Encapsulated in the book's subtitle 'The Extensions of Man', McLuhan argued that new 'cool' technologies extend our capabilities and enhance those aspects of practice which previously had been limited, either spatially or by time. However, at the same time new technologies swiftly naturalize such advances and make them seem 'everyday' rather than novel. While Machlup was seeking to quantify the economic changes engendered by new technologies in the early 1960s, McLuhan was already thinking about a technology-driven transformation of society. Society is often seen as the sum of the communications that take place within it, and the impact of technology on communications (and through communication, on society more generally) has therefore remained at the centre of much writing on the new age.

Mark Poster, for example, takes up McLuhan's famous notion that the 'medium is the message' and develops it further. Poster delineates three different 'modes of information', different ways of communicating knowledge and being in society, suggesting 'history may be periodized by variations in the structure' of the mode of information (1990: 6). Different ages have different ways of communicating and this will produce different societies. He tentatively identifies the main stages as 'face-to-face, orally mediated exchange;

written exchanges mediated by print; and electronically mediated exchange'. The first stage is 'characterized by symbolic correspondences, and the second stage is characterized by the representation of signs, [while] the third is characterized by informational simulations' (1990: 6). These stages are not consecutive: although each stage is historically later than the previous one, they do not replace each other but rather are superimposed. With the advent of new ICTs, not only has a new mode of information arrived ('electronically mediated' exchange) but also the two previous modes have had their character altered. Face-to-face communication is no longer limited by proximity, while signs can be represented (and recognized) across vast distances and enjoy much wider currency.

As 'each method of preserving and transmitting information profoundly intervenes in the networks of relationships that constitute a society', this has led to profound changes in society itself (Poster 1990: 7). Variations of this perspective on communication underpin much of the discussion of the information society. It is not only a shift in the character of contemporary society, not merely a shift in communicative methods within a society that remains broadly the same, it is something more. Or as Poster puts it: 'the solid institutional routines that have characterized modern society for some two hundred years are being shaken by the earthquake of electronically mediated communication and recomposed into new routines whose outlines are as yet by no means clear' (1990: 14). New societies, new communities (re)constructed through the use of ICTs will mean that the information society will be unlike the society from which it emerges. While there will be continuities, even these will be reshaped by the use and deployment of ICTs.

One of the key social shifts at the centre of writings on the information society is therefore the empowerment of individuals, and their communicative potential. In this new age of communications, Esther Dyson argues, we must disclose ourselves because by feeding into networks and sustaining them with relevant information, the benefits of membership will multiply; we should play an active role in existing communities or build our own; and we can offer our own 'products' across the net, helping ourselves and others (1997: 281–6). At the heart of the information society (as mediated by the internet) is a radical decentring of communication; individuals can remake their society by remaking their communication networks. However, since this decentring also allows for a fragmentation of real-life referents (job, physical appearance) which might constrain the construction of identity, Sherry Turkle argues that one of the key transformations heralded by the information society is the ability to (re)construct identity due to the (potential) anonymity of online communication (Turkle 1997). As a famous *New Yorker* cartoon of a dog at a computer once suggested: 'On the internet no one knows you are a dog.' We can, in other words, choose who we might be in these interactions, and we may be more than one person, presenting different 'selves' in different forums, freeing ourselves from social constraints.

From information society to network society

One stream of comment on the information society has been concerned with the transformation of society (and its economy), and a second stream has been concerned with the transformation of ourselves. Drawing both these streams of analysis together, Manuel Castells has proposed that ICTs have produced a new sort of society, the network society (1996, 1997a, 1998). It should be noted that Castells was hardly the first person to identify the importance of the network possibilities of widespread diffusion of ICTs. Indeed, nearly twenty years before it was at the centre of the French report on the *Computerization of Society* (Nora and Minc 1980), but Castells has undoubtedly made the term his own. I will not try to summarize Castells's influential work here, but I will briefly note some of the key themes which permeate his treatment of the information age.

Castells argues at length that the deployment of ICTs is producing a networked society, one where not only companies, but also individuals, can benefit from new communication capacities. Electronically mediated networks support the development and dissemination of knowledge and information, allowing the acceleration of adaptation and discovery. He also suggests, as have others, that developmental processes have shifted from being based on physical resources to an increased reliance on the mobilization and coordination of knowledge and information. This is leading to information capitalism and the network society. Summarizing his own argument, he suggests this shift is the result of three dynamics: the revolution in information technologies that has been accelerating since the 1970s; the post-1980 restructuring of capitalism, most significantly in its relation to the state; and the social movements which emerged in the 1960s and 1970s, and which continue to be important today, most significantly feminism and environmentalism

(Castells 1997b: 7). These dynamics prompted the emergence of the global information economy and a transformation of work, where labour has become less standardized, flexibility has become the norm, and the working class has been 'de-massified'.

Alongside these economic shifts are changes in societies' character. Throughout the three volumes Castells discusses the growing disparities in wealth that have been part of these developments. For Castells the information age is not an unalloyed good: the world is being brought closer together through the enhancement of communication, but there is also increasing evidence of social fragmentation and dislocation. In addition society has moved towards an obsession with the image (both in cultural affairs and politics) and a commercialization (or even enclosure) of the spaces of communication. The widespread deployment of ICTs has produced a new relation between time and space. Similar to many of the arguments around globalization, Castells proposes a new 'timeless time' and a 'space of flows': time is no longer subject to fixed sequencing and can be accumulated through information collection as well as annihilated through instantaneous communication across the world; the spatial construction of our world is now much more dependent on the flows of electronic pulses around networks (spaces which emerge through communal negotiation) than on mere physical locality. All of this leads to a new age, the information age. Certainly, Castells's work represents a more complex treatment of the information society, less subject to the overstatement elsewhere. Nevertheless, like others he makes a number of problematic claims which I scrutinize in the following chapters.

Four Central Claims about the Information Society

There is more than one way of distinguishing the different bases on which claims about the information society are made. For example, Frank Webster, in his comprehensive survey, distinguishes five approaches: the technological, the economic, the occupational, the spatial and the cultural, allocating particular accounts to each (1995: ch. 2). And for each of these approaches he recounts a negative and a positive story regarding the social effects of the information society: utopia or dystopia. Elsewhere, Alistair Duff delineates three ways of thinking about the information society: the information economic thesis; the information flows approach; and the information technology approach (2000: 170 and *passim*). However, I adopt a different procedure: I focus on four linked claims which figure prominently in most treatments of the emergence of the information society, and it is these which I interrogate in the rest of this book.

A social revolution

The most important claim in discussions of the information society is that a new age is being ushered in by new information technologies. In their 1978 report to the President of France, Simon Nora and Alain Minc argued: 'The computer is not the only technological innovation of recent years, but it does constitute the common factor that speeds the development of all others. Above all, insofar as it is responsible for an upheaval in the processing and storage of data, *it will alter the entire nervous system of social organization'* (1980: 3, emphasis added). The information society, driven by the new ICTs, represents a profound social revolution. Or, as Bill Gates surmised more recently, the 'global interactive network will transform our culture as dramatically as Gutenberg's press did the middle ages' (1996: 9). Relatively ubiquitous computing (networked through the internet) will have ramifications similar to those of the printing revolution. In another frequent comparison, the computer revolution is 'at least as major a historical event as was the eighteenth-century Industrial Revolution, inducing a pattern of discontinuity in the material basis of economy, society and culture' (Castells 1996: 30). Thus it is broadly comparable to two previous 'revolutions', the emergence of printing, and the transformation of industrial organization. Furthermore, Nicholas Negroponte suggests it is irreversible: 'Like a force of nature, the digital age cannot be stopped' (1995: 229). This common perception of inevitability linked to the recognition of profound changes prompted by the information society leads many to argue that we are entering a new age: the information age.

There are a number of problems with these overarching claims for revolution (which I explore at length in the next chapter). Most obviously they involve a view of society that assumes a major determining role for technology. Indeed, technology is perceived as imposing its character on the rest of society. However, technologies are developed in specific social circumstances and deployed reflecting contemporary social relations. The relationship between technology, its 'character' and society is much more complex than a unidirectional determinism allows. Furthermore, many of the claims for revolution telescope the history of information technologies to identify profound changes on the basis of the most recent generations of ICTs. Once we recognize that there has been a long gestation of the relevant technologies and of their interaction with societies across the globe, then the claims for revolution start to look a little strained. However, within such claims there are three other elements which are problematic in their own right.

The new economy

A second set of claims introduces the much discussed 'new economy'. At the centre of the 'Californian ideology' which underlies much writing regarding the information economy is the notion that 'existing social, political and legal power structures will wither away to be replaced by unfettered interactions between autonomous individuals' (Barbrook and Cameron 1996: 53). The workforce of the information economy will no longer be a single definable group (or 'class') but rather a fragmented network of individual contractors. There is a new division of labour encapsulated in the rise of outsourcing and project-based contracts at the expense of long-term company employment, as well as the increase of service sector employment relative to manufacturing jobs. This rise of services has been represented as a move to a 'weightless economy', one in which the products are not physical but rather informational (hence weightless). 'These days most people in most advanced economies produce nothing that can be weighed: communications, software, advertising, financial services. They trade, write, design, talk, spin and create: rarely do they make anything' (Leadbeater 1999: 18). The argument is clear: in this new information economy we work primarily with our minds rather than with our hands, and these jobs are best understood as service related, as the provision of information, the deployment of knowledge. Work has been transformed, there has been a move to more flexible working practices which enable workers to trade more easily on their expertise and skills. In this new economy it is ideas that count, knowledge that is the important resource.

In chapter 3 I examine these claims and argue that, while they describe some elements of recent shifts in work practices, they miss considerable continuities and actually hide a return to some rather familiar practices. The new economy, while clearly evident for some workers, is limited in extent and reach. Indeed, the employment statistics which are often used to demonstrate these shifts do not support the conclusions drawn from them. Furthermore, in the real world of service work, past employment practices (including surveillance and control) are still exercised by managers and employers, and in some instances have even been enhanced by ICTs. To a large extent the continuity of economic relations in the 'new economy' has been supported by the successful expansion of property rights in information and knowledge. Much about the new economy is therefore not new at all.

Information politics

In the pre-internet discussion of the information society, the transformation of politics and community focused on the rise of experts and the power they might enjoy (as in Bell 1974). Marc Porat, for instance, claimed that 'the manager-scientist-professional is the new knight, absorbing the old powers of the capitalist, the landlord, the general and the priest' (1978: 79). The controller of knowledge and information, the technocrat, would replace the rule of wealth, landed estates, military power and religion that had typified previous societies. But as ICTs became more and more widely available in the 1990s, the possibility of new politically active 'communities' became a central theme of writing on the information society. These communities would be 'independent of geography' and individuals could belong to many cyber-communities related to their different political interests and with varying levels of commitment (Dyson 1997: 32–3). Thus, not only are new social groups appearing but they will mobilize widely dispersed individuals into effective (niche) interest groups who will have an increasing impact on the political process. In this sense, the 'new social movements' are emblematic of political community in the information age. Mobilizing on the basis of arguments for the transformation of personal lives, as well as political interest, a new networked politics is emerging.

This suggests that the character of democratic accountability and participation in the information age is changing. While there remain problems of access and the control of any putative public space on the internet, here I am a little less sceptical of the veracity of claims for change. There does seem to be a shift in the manner of political activity. However, while pressure groups and political campaigns have certainly deployed ICTs extensively, it is a lot less easy to substantiate their political efficacy. And although the state retains a central political role, many governments have found it difficult (or have been unwilling) to construct new forms of interaction with their citizens, and have instead continued to rely on their existing, tried and tested networks. Some political problems have also been enhanced by the arrival of the information society, of which the two most often recognized concern privacy and censorship. In chapter 4 I examine the claims for the transformation of community and the character of political life, but these arguments also lead to the fourth key claim about the information society I want to discuss.

The decline of the state

An underlying distrust of government in the discussion of information society often takes the form of an explicit argument that it will allow civil society to successfully confront the state, which is outdated and no longer (if it ever was) the most efficient way to organize society. While this does not necessarily suggest their complete dissolution, states will 'have to become more open as the old hierarchical bureaucracies are becoming irrelevant to the new generation' (Tapscott 1998: 265, 290). There may be a residual role for centralized political authority but this is much diminished in the information age. But states may try to hold on to power, and therefore democracy becomes a struggle against their continuing domination of society. Conversely, it is argued, the power of the state to intervene has in any case been fatally compromised by ICTs. Here arguments regarding the state in a world patterned by the globalization of social, political and economic relations come into play. Although states have never been able to claim a monopoly of power in the domestic political economy, the 'information revolution' has undermined the state's ability to control information for its own ends, with fatal consequences for its overall authority. While some states still make strong claims for authority (despite *and* because of ICTs), in general the state is being challenged by the information society in many areas where its authority has been relatively uncontested for at least a century.

I argue in the fifth chapter that although the decline of the state is a death frequently foretold, the end is hardly imminent. Not only have some states been very successful at organizing their economies to respond to the information revolution, the supposition that such a revolution can transpire without a central role for the state is mistaken. Much of the analysis of the information society reifies the market by ignoring the crucial role of legal institutions in capitalist society. More importantly, given the dependence of the new economy on intellectual property rights, without strong state authority the economy of the information society would be unworkable. More generally, only by obscuring the role of law and authority in society can proclamations of the information age suppose the state must necessarily be in decline. Although their role is changing, states continue to be crucial to the societies they govern.

If not now, when?

In the following chapters I take each of these four key arguments, explore them in more detail and suggest some shortcomings in their depiction of the 'new age'. I am not suggesting these are the only claims which could be made about the information society, but they seem to me to be the central themes of the contemporary debate. The literature focusing on the information society has been developed over at least thirty years, and in the 1970s and 1980s quite a large literature of criticism was evident. Some of these earlier critiques appear in subsequent chapters and help me develop my criticism of the more recent claims about the information society. One of the reasons for writing this book is that recently, while some of the possible consequences of the information age have been subject to quite intensive political debate, the assumption that it represents a transformation of society itself is now regarded as relatively unproblematic. Utopians have been confronted by dystopians, but both accept that we are self-evidently entering a new age.

In this book I want to question whether our contemporary society is entering this new age, or whether, while there are some important changes we can recognize, the continuities are more profound. Given the length of time that the information society has supposedly been imminent, the argument that these things 'will come to pass' in the future is a prediction that is increasingly difficult to sustain. If there are few signs of a wholesale transformation of society in a period when the deployment of ICTs is accelerating, then it is unlikely that these four claims can really be substantiated. Again, I want to stress, I am not arguing that there are no changes that can be linked to, or may even be caused by the widening use of ICTs. However, when we strip away changes in the superficial forms that interactions in the information society take, we find considerable continuity of substance. And while, as I have already noted, this is a simplistic way of putting the more complex and nuanced argument of the following chapters, this distinction is still important for our understanding of contemporary society.

2

Locating the 'Information Age' in History

Central to many proclamations of the arrival of the (global) information society is a story about history. As Cees Hamelink put it some years ago, 'a powerful myth is being persuasively told by numerous story-tellers. It is the myth of the information society . . . It suggests that the "information revolution" is the most significant historical development of our time: a revolutionary transition to a fundamentally different age' (1986: 7). Although in the intervening years the myth's profile has ebbed and flowed, with the acceleration of internet connectivity it has become ever more widely retold. Before I discuss the three central claims that make up this myth, it is as well to examine its more general form: that the emergence of the information society is revolutionary in character, heralding a new (information) age.

The meaning of 'revolution' was diluted during the twentieth century with all sorts of sectoral shifts heralded as 'revolutions' (the 'shopping revolution', the 'education revolution', and so on). Previously, it had been a term used to identify profound and complete transformations of society produced by political action (the English or French Revolutions) or by large-scale economic change (the agricultural or industrial revolutions) (Williams 1976: 226–30). In the early nineteenth century (during industrialization), invocations of 'revolutionary' technological development were 'taken out of the realm of history proper and equipped with the mantle of ideology, or myth. It became not just a description of certain linked structural changes in society, but a rallying-cry, a programme for action, a justification of the inevitable harshnesses that must accompany the effort to industrialise' (Kumar 1978: 47). It is this notion of (industrial) revolution as myth, or an ideology of mobilization, which has been taken up in the writing on the information society.

Like these previous declarations, at the same time as arguing the revolution is happening, writers frequently have instructed us how we can further its actualization. Previous technological revolutions have been often presented as unavoidable but ultimately socially beneficial. Regarded as the sign of progress, new technologies were 'assumed to produce, almost as a by-product, the liberation of the human spirit' (Slack 1984: 251). This led Jennifer Slack to argue that, like previous revolutions, the information revolution is presented as if technology itself were autonomous. This is meant to encourage us to place ourselves in a particular relationship with the revolution's constituent technologies: as users, not creators; reacting to rather than rejecting. Thus the idea of technological revolution may reveal not only possible changes in society, but also the ideological or political importance of making such claims.

The myth of the information revolution helps naturalize the phenomenon it describes, presenting criticism as mere misunderstanding. Thus, for instance, John Naisbitt was surprised in 1984 that 'so many people passionately resist the notion of an economy built on information, and, *despite a wealth of evidence*, deny the industrial era is over' (1984: 11, emphasis added). But since then this naturalization has been so successful that criticisms of the information revolution's revolutionary credentials have been increasingly marginalized. Nowadays we argue about the implications of the changes but *not* their 'reality'. And therefore Don Tapscott was able to claim: 'Such extreme characterizations don't arise because the world acquired a new taste for hyperbole. Rather language flows from the attempts of baffled business leaders, boggled academics and amazed journalists to somehow characterize the world we are entering and how the changes underway are unlike anything before' (1996: 4). From this perspective the assertion of an information revolution is not exaggeration, it is merely the attempt to understand enormous changes in society.

The widespread discussion of the 'information age' reinforces these claims of transformation, and means to establish an important division in history, like that marked by the older meaning of 'revolution'. As used by the historian Eric Hobsbawm, for instance, previous ages (the ages of Revolution, Capital and Empire) gave way to the 'Age of Extremes' in the twentieth century (Hobsbawm 1994). The use of the term 'age', like 'revolution' before it, tells us something about what is intended by a specific analysis: 'An age connotes an all-pervasive logic, a logic that requires that everything be explained in its own terms . . . The information age thus hails all subjects as trapped in its logic' (Slack 1984: 253). And certainly, there has been no shortage of assertions of a new age ushered in by the widespread use of powerful new information and communication technologies (ICTs) which has profoundly changed the logic of social existence. The central claim in accounts of the (global) information society is that it is a revolutionary new age, and this claim has been set out in a number of ways.

The New Age

In 1970 this new age was still on the horizon, but as we accelerated towards it, we seemed about to 'face an abrupt collision with the future' (Toffler 1970: 18). Even in the middle of the decade, Daniel Bell still saw much of his 'venture in social forecasting' as speculative in character; the new age remained indeterminate. By taking note of his predictions, social actors could shape and control the future (Bell 1974). But by the 1980s the new age was dawning. Wilson Dizard suggested that the move to an information society was not 'simply a linear extension of what has gone on before . . . [but] a qualitative shift in the thrust and purpose' of society. After labelling it, we needed to face the fact that 'the current shift appears to be a departure from the dynamics that drove our agricultural and industrial past' (Dizard 1982: 2, 182–3). Nevertheless, at this point it seemed that the revolution could still be shaped, controlled or channelled, and analyses usually allowed some place for government direction and planning (which I will return to in chapter 5). However, the notion that we might have some (political) control over the direction of the information revolution has since faded. The information society has become a wave which we can surf but cannot change. One of the ways this shift from engagement to passive accommodation has been accomplished is by presenting these changes as epochal rather than merely taking place *within* contemporary society.

One of the most influential treatments of the epochal story was presented by Alvin Toffler, who encapsulated the information age as a third wave (Toffler 1980). He has continued to write about the new age (Toffler and Toffler 1993), and through his contacts with American policy-makers (and political foundations) has had a major impact on the way the information society has been thought about in the United States and elsewhere. Indeed, the 'third wave' finds its way into much that is written about the information society, having attained the position of 'received truth'. Essentially Toffler's argument is that there have been two previous revolutions or waves in the way humans have organized their economic affairs (the agricultural and industrial), and now the information revolution is a third. Our existence was revolutionized in prehistory by the emergence of the technologies of farming, as opposed to hunting and gathering, leading to the key shift to plant-and-grow rather than merely to search for and find food. Around the seventeenth and eighteenth centuries the industrial revolution started to gather pace (building on, and part of, the scientific revolution), finally taking full advantage of the surpluses and knowledge that had slowly been developed since the first wave.

The second wave could never have happened without the transformation of the first wave, and likewise, the third wave can only get under way now because of the major achievements of the second wave (Toffler 1980). The deployment and use of increasingly powerful ICTs is the key driver of the third wave in the same way as emergent farming and industrial technologies spurred the previous waves. The heightened productivity that was produced by the utilization of farming technologies enabled a surplus over and above subsistence levels of production as expertise and experience grew. This freed some people from the land and allowed them to devote time and effort to building social institutions. In the industrial second wave, the organization of production in factories enabled a further leap in productivity, by shifting vast numbers of men and women into jobs where they no longer produced discrete products but rather were organized to perform specialist tasks. This new division of labour then prompted further specialization and additional increases in productivity. The first wave allowed society to grow from the relatively small dispersed groups who had previously roamed the world, into semi-urbanized societies where cultural and social innovation emerged. Industrialization eventually widened the benefits of these activities to groups previously excluded or at least marginalized, and accelerated the development of science, technology and culture.

As with the previous two waves, when we emerge from the transitional period, society will have been remade. This remaking is reflected in the way states interact (Toffler and Toffler 1993), in the way society is organized and in the sorts of economic activities which will be valued and provide employment (Toffler 1980). Underlying this perspective (whether it is explicitly drawn from Toffler, or not) is a combination of the notion of 'creative destruction' originally developed by Joseph Schumpeter to describe the way capitalism moved forward by rendering redundant the technologies that preceded current developments, and Nikolai Kondratieff's idea that the global economy moved through 'long waves' of economic development. Joining these ideas together produces a notion of periods of upheaval (related to technological change) between long waves.

This leads writers such as Nicholas Negroponte to argue that the information age is a natural force which brooks no resistance. These shifts, whether welcome or not, are unavoidable. Indeed David Brown argues in *Cybertrends* that the 'current, *technically induced reconfiguration* of the world economy will pose profound concerns not only about the future of most human livelihoods but also about individual and social identity, and about the very future of democracy itself' (1997: 10–11, emphasis added). The character of the world is being transformed, but not by negotiation; rather it is 'technically induced', it is out of our hands. Diane Coyle suggests technology may be used in ways we cannot yet predict but that this shift is inevitable or 'inexorable' (1997: 23). Furthermore, the new age has been universalized. While there may be vast disparities in the world, we are continually told that the form of society which all countries need to aspire to if they are to enjoy continued economic and social development is the information society. And even if they cannot fully informationalize now, even if they are yet to deploy new ICTs extensively, the logic of this transformation of the global system will eventually revolutionize all societies in any case. The depiction of the information age becomes the explicit expression of inevitability, of normality, of progress.

Looking at these arguments which assert the dawning of a new age, there are two elements which need to be examined before moving to the more focused discussions which follow. There is the important question of what differentiates this new era from its predecessor; what changes are presented as demonstrating a new age. We need to have an idea of how the previous age might be characterized so we can compare it with the new. But first we need to examine the supposed causes of these profound changes: what is causing the revolution?

Technological Determinism and the Information Age

Those who proclaim that the development and deployment of new ICTs have produced profound changes in society start from the premise that technological changes bring in their wake major shifts in the societies which use them. Indeed, to argue that ICTs are producing a new age *requires* this assumption, as otherwise it would make little sense to place such explanatory weight on ICTs. The use of information and knowledge is as old as society itself. Therefore, even analyses which explicitly focus on the changes in the uses and/or types of information (and knowledge) that pattern society still assume it is new information technologies which allow the new uses identified as transformative. This position implies that our previous history was also determined by the development of technology: no one has argued (as far as I am aware) that ICTs are the first technologies ever to produce a major impact on the history of society. The argument for the emergence of the information society therefore also involves a general claim about historical processes.

The notion that technology is an independent causal factor in history is hardly new. As Langdon Winner notes in his classic study *Autonomous Technology* (1978), the perception of autonomous technological development has frequently become the fear of 'technology out-of-control' in political debates. The identification of a technological imperative combines the recognition of actual processes of change in technologies with the suggestion that humankind's common disposition is to react and accommodate change, not to try and reverse or redirect it. When joined together in arguments about technology, 'the process and the disposition create what can be called technological dynamism, a forceful movement in history which continues largely without human guidance' (Winner 1978: 105). By linking a recognition of changes in technology with an assumption of human inaction in the face of such changes, the role of technology in history becomes magnified into technological determinism. By taking changes in technology as the most important single factor in explaining any particular change in society, technological determinists deny (or ignore) the role of social and political choice, obscuring the social embeddedness of technology.

It is especially ironic that ICTs should be embraced and the demands which they put on us meekly accepted while at the same time suspicion of scientific and technical advances in other areas seems to be growing (witness the plight of genetically modified organisms in the food market). This may reflect the length of time that the information revolution seems to be taking; the technology is no longer that new. Indeed, Don Tapscott suggests that the use and effects of new ICTs have already become second nature to a new generation, for whom computers are not *new* technologies but just part of the world into which they were born (1998: 38 and *passim*). We may already be used to these technologies, and so are less suspicious of them than recent developments in biotechnology. The idea that biotechnology is out of control is widespread and much discussed, although the problem of technological determinism figures as much in those debates as it does in the arguments about the information society. However, while many authors have been accused of technological determinism, it is those concerned with the emergence of the information society I am interested in.

Ian Angell's dystopian *New Barbarian Manifesto*, for instance, opens with the statement that 'a "brave new world" is being forced upon unsuspecting societies by advances in information technology' (2000: v). Technology has a life of its own, its impact is set by its nature and as such it must be accommodated by society; first there is technological change and then there is history. This is not an unusual or novel view. Frank Webster has concluded that 'for those who assert that we are witnessing the emergence of an "information society", high on their list of shared principles is technological determinism' (1995: 219). Technological determinists tend to think (to varying degrees) that technological advances happen automatically, that there is a logic to technological developments which is outside our control.

There are three possible strands of technological determinism – the normative; the nomological; and accounts that stress unintended consequences (Bimber 1995) – and most accounts of the information society have elements of one or more within them. In the normative approach, particular technologies embody specific norms (like efficiency or democracy) which are automatically promoted through the deployment and use of the technology concerned. In recent accounts of the information society, for instance, the technologies of the internet are often judged to embody the norm of 'freedom of expression' encapsulated in the First Amendment to the US constitution, or are said to encourage the global development of democracy and resistance to tyranny. Other more radical accounts have suggested that, almost unwittingly, the internet and its associated technologies have promoted 'cyber-communism' or a gift economy. This is seen as part of the logic of the internet *despite* its origins and use in a capitalist economy (Barbrook 2000). However, Bruce Bimber argues, while often included in broad characterizations of technological determinism, these norm-centred approaches allow some interaction with non-technological norms which are socially determined. Thus they should not be regarded as fully deterministic even when they allow little space for mediation and modification of these technological norms, as the norms themselves find their roots in society not technology.

Currently, few positive accounts of the information age stress its unintended consequences, not least of all because so much effort is spent predicting the 'new age' in all its variants. Most consequences are regarded as intentional, following from the widespread deployment of ICTs by companies and other groups expecting to benefit from such consequences. Critics of the information age on the other hand have been more inclined to identify seemingly unexpected outcomes ranging from issues broadly collected under the rubric of the 'digital divide' (new social cleavages introduced by the use of ICTs) to the enhanced possibility of theft/piracy of intellectual assets by digitalization, or through the erosion of privacy by new modes of surveillance. The criticisms I make later in the book also reflect such unintended consequences: I suggest social structures have been reinforced rather than demolished. But this may only be seen as unintended by those proclaiming a new age. They can hardly be said to be completely unintended by those in powerful positions who have supported the deployment of ICTs in various areas of our lives. However, again as Bimber points out, accounts which stress unintended consequences while accepting some sort of technological momentum really cannot be deterministic, because to be deterministic the outcomes would have had to have been foreseeable. For unintended outcomes to develop there must be a mediating role for some other factor, which for ease we might call society.

This leaves the nomological approach (for Bimber, the only 'true' technological determinism). Here accounts stress the independence of technology, and focus on its logical development from one innovation to the next. As Bimber puts it, this is built on two linked claims: 'that technological developments occur according to some naturally given logic, which is not culturally or socially determined, and that these developments force social adaptation and changes' (1995: 84). In this perspective, technology is treated as responding to natural laws of development, and society must adapt to its contours. A classic example of this sort of logic is the elevation of 'Moore's Law', regarding the doubling of computer chip capacities every eighteen months, from observation to predictive device.

Predictions of this sort have led Brian Loader to conclude that much that is written about the information society adopts an apolitical attitude towards technological development. Thus to 'question the possible consequences of such technological innovation for social structures and economic activity is often regarded as at best having a negative "mindset" and at worst to be labelled a Luddite' (Loader 1998: 6).

However, looking back, this might not be quite the insult intended. The Luddites were far from mistaken in their analyses of the immediate impact of technology. Despite the arguments arrayed against them, despite the accusations that they failed to realize the long-term benefits of the introduction of new machines into the textile industry, they were proved largely correct in their analysis of the immediate consequences of technical change. After all, as E. P. Thompson pointed out, 'it is impossible to designate as "progressive", in any meaningful sense, processes which brought about the degradation, for twenty or thirty years ahead, of the workers employed in the industry' (1980: 603). While the urge to smash computers is unlikely to be converted into widespread and organized direct action, as I argue later in this chapter, there is a need to recognize that the information society represents a repetition of a process that has been an integral part of capitalism's history.

Any form of technological determinism may lead to an absence of concern for the effects of the information revolution in terms of justice and equity, as well as a denial of politics. Margaret Archer argues that this must be refuted: 'the attempt to avoid moral philosophical concerns by making technology the means to achieve mankind's desires cannot deem any and all outcomes to be progress' if we are to try and construct 'the *Good Society*' (1990: 112). If we are to resist both strong and weak determinism, we need to establish that there is nothing fixed or certain about the effects technologies may have on society; technologies (including ICTs) are not natural nor autonomous. As Raymond Williams argued in relation to television, any 'new technology is itself a product of a particular social system, and will be developed as an apparently autonomous process of innovation only to the extent we fail to identify and challenge its real agencies' (1974: 135). Technology is itself a political phenomenon and thus the information age is not the unavoidable consequence of technological developments.

To maintain that a particular argument is (at least partly) technologically deterministic is not to suggest that any changes it identifies are meaningless, rather it is to dispute an argument which presumes all major changes in society are driven by technological developments. It is this argument, that technology is the single most important cause of changes in our society, which is the major problem with the literature that identifies and promotes the information society. One way of trying to dissolve this problem is to rethink the way we conceive of the history of technology itself by utilizing the work of Lewis Mumford, who, although often regarded as the father of the study of the history of technology, always argued strenuously against technological determinism.

Lewis Mumford and Technological History

Lewis Mumford's perspective on the history of technology suggests how the information revolution can be seen as part of this history, rather than as a revolution separate from it (May 2000c). Utilizing Mumford's ideas about technology, relatively recent developments in ICTs become (or remain) part of a continuing history of technological development, and by understanding the dynamics of this history we can illuminate the debates over the consequences and character of the information revolution.

Mumford's perspective focused on the importance of 'symbolic activities' and their relation to technology. He firmly resisted the exclusively material analysis of technical advance, which links a series of technologies in a 'progressive' history with little regard for their symbolic importance. According to Mumford, the 'constant danger in interpreting human behaviour is to overvalue exact methods and measurable data, separated from their historical context' (1962: 202). While such evidence should not itself be dismissed, it needed to be joined with the social factors which he thought historians too often dismissed. Technological history is not merely the progress through improvement and innovation from one technology to another, but rather is an ongoing interaction between the material and the symbolic, between material technology and its social meaning and its use (Mumford 1971: 421–9). Therefore, we can only understand the history of technology by (re)embedding it in the societies where this history unfolds. The artefacts which could be uncovered and investigated in the quest for this history have consistently skewed the narratives of technology towards an overemphasis on its material aspects relative to social factors and the ideas which encourage particular trajectories of technological advance (but of which firm evidence remains sparse).

Our relation with technology is not as passive receiver of innovation: humans shape the social context which produces technological advance. Our ideas and concerns are major factors in the history of technology, and are not merely *caused* by this history. Mumford stressed human agency in the history of technology and frequently focused on the danger of allowing ourselves to be controlled by technology rather than shaping it. To emphasize this social context, Mumford discussed 'technics' rather than technology. This term encapsulates his perception of the importance of our interaction with technology: technologies should be located within their social relations, their context, before assessing their logic and effect. Historically, technics have reflected two contradictory dynamics, which Mumford termed authoritarian and democratic (May 2000c: 248–53). This distinction does not relate to *specific* technologies, but rather the use to which particular technologies are put (and their developmental trajectory) locate them broadly in one or other of these dynamics. Technics are the combination of technology and its social organization. Centralizing authority tries to control the use and outputs of technology, but is unable to completely micromanage the society which it governs. A space for resistance remains available where technologies may emancipate and empower individuals *against* the authoritarian power. It is this possibility which supports and reproduces democratic technics.

Authoritarian and democratic technics

For Mumford, authoritarian technics first emerged during the period of pyramid building in Egypt. Collecting together vast mega-machines of organic components (men, women and children) to do their bidding, utilizing the new skills of communication including writing, mathematics and bureaucratic control, the 'God Kings' constructed structures that were beyond the capabilities of previous societies. In a sense, the ability to organize large groups of people to specific ends marks the dawn of 'civilization' in Mumford's eyes, even if such civilization brought with it the problem of authority and domination. However, this first wave of authoritarian technics (at its height with the Roman Empire) could only support the emergence of new technologies in urban centres.

Mumford argued that these first authoritarian technics finally proved too dependent on the centre retaining control: once communication failed and authority was no longer regarded as legitimate, the mega-machine(s) collapsed. Democratic technics could then assert themselves during the Middle Ages, when small-scale technologies allowed the development of localized societies, free from the domination of an authoritarian bureaucracy demanding service or tribute. While such freedom was variable and insecure, it was in any case subsequently again constrained by the rise of the nation-state, the mega-machine *par excellence*.

As the rule of the state began to be consolidated in Europe, the Enlightenment and the scientific revolution led to a view that technological development and scientific progress would produce an increasingly democratic society. But this hope was dashed by the return of authoritarian technics in the form of the widening technological apparatus of the modern state in industrialized capitalism.

> At the very moment Western nations threw off the ancient regime of absolute government, operating under a once-divine king, they were restoring this same system in a far more effective form in their technology, reintroducing coercions of a military character no less strict in the organisation of a factory than in that of the new drilled, uniformed, army. (Mumford 1964: 4)

The powerful had constructed a system in which technology supported their claims for omnipotence. Most importantly for Mumford, technological deployment and its effects reflect these social relations: *no* technology is beyond systemic incorporation into authoritarian technics.

Under this system of authoritarian technics there is no longer a sovereign location of power: it is the system itself that actualizes authority. It is the system that sets the limits to action (and possibility) rather than an actual (locatable) ruler, and this helps authority defuse much of the continuing resistance flowing from democratic technics. While there are still powerful groups and individuals, their role is largely masked by their ability to define their needs as the technological system's 'natural' needs. The system maintains its domination by providing for the majority an abundance of material goods without historical precedent. But this is only possible where non-systemic wants are not articulated, and where only deliverable demands are acceptable. Therefore authoritarian technics are always vulnerable to democratic technics.

For Mumford it is self-discovery, the ability of human beings to change, that always undermines the ability of authoritarian technics to retain control without constant (and contested) reproduction. The bribe of abundance and material wealth offered by authoritarian technics in return for a narrowing of human potential and a decline in psychological health *can* be rejected. It is imperative, Mumford argues, that the human scale of life be central to democracy; society must revolve around humans not the system (Mumford 1964: 8). Thus, while technology is itself neither authoritarian nor democratic, it must be *positively* integrated into democratic technics; its democratic potential will not emerge without effort and social action. In contrast to authoritarian technics, democratic technics are localized and 'even when employing machines, remain under the active direction of the craftsman', responding to their needs and wants (Mumford 1964: 3). They have modest demands (which is to say localized power needs, readily available skills, low organizational requirements) and can be adapted to local conditions. More importantly they remain under the *control* of the local user. Democratic technics retain (or recapture) a level of autonomy, and thus allow local creativity to be exercised.

Furthermore, Mumford claimed, democratic technics free the individual from the burden of continual employment, allowing the development of non-system oriented behaviour. He proposed the emancipation of the creative individual: democratic technics allow work that is dependent on 'special skill, knowledge, aesthetic sense'. Large-scale enterprise may continue, but a space for individual expression through artisanal activities within the localized community must be retained. The development of self can continue under democratic technics, even if selfhood is stifled by the demands of authoritarian technics. Indeed the notion that technology should abolish all work is far from Mumford's mind: 'work which is not confined to the muscles, but incorporates all of the functions of the mind, is not a curse but a blessing' (1966b: 242). However, to gain these benefits, passivity in the face of technology is useless: although democratic technics potentially exist, they need to be positively constructed.

Technologies have no natural character; they do not automatically support or destroy democracy, but rather help reproduce social structures and systems through the manner in which they are used (and misused). Put simply, authoritarian technics utilize technology in a manner which enhances the ability of top-down rule over society, while democratic technics enable the relative autonomy of local groups and enhance their ability to produce bottom-up innovations and movement in society. Consequently, democratic technics and authoritarian technics do not replace one another, but rather exist side-by-side, in competition, ebbing and flowing but never finally erased. They will often use the same technologies, but in very different ways. Thus the resistance to capitalism using its own technologies, such as recent 'reclaim the streets' protests organized through chat-rooms and newsgroups/email, or the increasingly widespread disregard of music copyright by users of MP3 files accessed through Napster and other programs, fits Mumford's notion of the reassertion of democratic technics rather well.

The two technics in the information age

Mumford's notion of two contrasting technics, authoritarian and democratic, runs parallel to the distinction that often divides opinion regarding the information society: whether its dynamic is 'disclosing' or 'enclosing' (May 2000c: 257–61). On each side of this argument, one dynamic is regarded as normal while the other is regarded as a temporary aberration which will wither as the information society continues to develop. This contrasting of normal and abnormal results in a widespread reproduction of partial perspectives on the information society, which lapse into casual technological determinism by refusing to acknowledge the mediated and indeterminate progress of the 'information revolution'. Each side assumes that its dynamic identifies the *real* character of the information society. Any contradictory aspects of these shifts are temporary and will be resolved by the triumph of the technological logic they have identified.

Those who identify an enclosing dynamic suggest that the information society involves an intensification of property relations, the increasing ownership of knowledge in various forms. The ability to render knowledge and information as intellectual property rights (IPRs) suggests that the information society represents an expansion of modern capitalism. (In the appendix I set out what intellectual property is.) In these arguments, social organization is defined and understood on the basis of the raw materials which are the subject of economic activity (along with the organizational structures of such activities). This has not been profoundly altered by the rise and expansion of the information economy. The ability of economic actors to treat new forms of products and services as (intellectual) property suggests continuity not disjuncture, and I return to this issue in the next section when I discuss commodification. However, not all who describe an enclosing dynamic see this as a problem; on the contrary some commentators (for example, Bill Gates or Peter Drucker) expect the deployment of ICTs in a capitalist framework to enhance and improve capitalism. Where knowledge is made property, this will make its use more efficient and support the ability of intellectual workers to be rewarded for their efforts, thereby encouraging further development of the knowledge that drives the information society.

For the enclosing dynamic therefore, ICTs and the information economy will reproduce current social organization while making it faster and more 'efficient'. In its critical mode, this perspective rejects arguments for the 'new economy', seeing it merely as capitalist business as usual. As this is unlikely to reduce concentrations of power (indeed it may further the centralization of society), this fits well with the characterization of authoritarian technics in Mumford's work, and the identification of the centralizing and controlling aspects of technological development. The role of system-as-ruler is fulfilled by the 'logic' of capitalist socioeconomic organization. Any aspects of the information revolution which do not conform to this path (such as piracy or non-commercial use of ICTs) will fade because they do not represent the revolution's true logic. But while this characterization of the information age may reflect much that is happening, this is only one side of the story.

Arrayed against those who regard the information society as exhibiting an enclosing dynamic are those who regard the information revolution as leading to expansive human empowerment. This competing perception suggests that the information society exhibits a disclosing dynamic: the information age will enhance and extend the availability of (free) information and as such will transform our information-dependent lives. The discussion of the information society has often taken this democratic or disclosing logic as characteristic of the newest developments in ICTs such as the explosion in internet usage. Writers such as John Perry Barlow recognize that property in information resources is increasingly difficult to sustain; indeed it represents exactly the type of control the information society is undermining. The disclosing dynamic is normalized and the enclosing tendencies are represented as a threat or abnormality which will be overcome: 'information wants to be free' and resistance is pointless. Information society will be built on inter-personal relations rather than through property relations (Barlow 1996; Tapscott 1998; Barbrook 2000). Individuals will be equipped to engage with each other through the widespread deployment of ICTs and network connectivity, leading to a new democratic society free from unnecessary authority.

The information society, conceived as democratic technics, allows individuals to express themselves outside mass parties and outside class identities (claims investigated in chapter 4). This is the result of the vast expansion in the information resources available for individuals to make such choices. Gone is the control of information by the expert; rather we can all access the information we need without the mediation of others. Information will dissolve the threads of power and make hierarchies increasingly difficult to maintain, not only in democracies but throughout the global system (Cleveland 1985). Politics will be more concerned with people than geography, issues – not class – will become the mainstay of political interaction. In his much cited trilogy on *The Information Age*, Manuel Castells suggests that politics is coalescing around symbolic issues (the environment, human rights) which are driven by the disclosure of abuses previously obscured (1997a: 309ff.). In Mumford's terms, democratic technics, allowing communal self-government, free communication between equals and unimpeded access to the common store of knowledge, are (re)emerging through ICTs' ability to make such flows a reality where previously they might have been obstructed by the structures of industrial society. Again, the con-flicting dynamic (here of enclosure) is presented as abnormal and transitory, at odds with the 'real' defining character of the informa-tion society.

Lewis Mumford's key insight is that actually these two dynam-ics are not contradictory: both are continuing elements of the history of technology and its social milieu. The move to control and enclose (authoritarian technics in their systemic mode) exists alongside the tendency to escape control and disclose (democratic technics). For Mumford the history of technology has been a process of interac-tion and conflict between democratic and authoritarian technics, not the technological progression finally towards one or the other. Technics have not been the result of specific technologies but are the product of the social, political and economic relations in which tech-nologies appear, are developed and deployed. The importance of this insight is that it enables us to see that while there are many arguments about new technologies and developments, they represent only a further phase of a technological history, the clash of technics which has been continuing since we first learnt to articulate thought through language (for Mumford, humankind's first technological revolution). This approach to the history of technology suggests that the contemporary arguments about the role of ICTs in social relations are the latest chapter in a long story.

The sceptical view of the information society which I lay out in this book should not be confused with an assertion that the enclosing dynamic is characteristic of the information age. Rather, with Mumford's insight in mind, I aim to (re)establish a perspective on the 'information age' which accepts that the tension between authoritarian and democratic technics, or between enclosing and disclosing dynamics, cannot be resolved. This lack of final resolution is the key to understanding changes within, and the development of, the information society. As the subsequent chapters reveal, there are elements of the information age that reflect each set of technics or dynamic. If at times I seem to favour the recognition of an overarching authoritarian dynamic, this is only meant to encourage the development and valuing of democratic technics by recognizing the danger of authoritarian technics. It is explicitly *not* an argument that authoritarian technics are an inevitable outcome of the information age. That said, I now move to discuss the central contention of the enclosing dynamic, that the information society is merely capitalism remade.

Marx, Capitalism and the Information Society

In this section I deploy aspects of Karl Marx's analysis to identify some important central elements of capitalism as an organizational practice. While Marx recognized that there were differing forms of capitalism, he was interested in exploring the elements these variants shared (Hodgson 1999: 117ff.). Despite being diagnosed from an analysis of the historical particulars of nineteenth-century capitalism, these elements remain central to the economic organization of the information age. This indicates that the information society does not imply a fundamentally new way of organizing the economy, but is rather another (albeit recently emerging) form of capitalist society. Nevertheless, some have argued we are moving towards a new information capitalism, unlike its predecessor in important aspects (Drucker 1993; Leadbeater 1999). In the press this has sometimes been referred to as the 'new paradigm', or more recently the 'new economy'. To assess this sort of claim we need at least to have an outline understanding of the defining characteristics of capitalism. The argument that the information revolution has transformed the organization of economic activity *within* capitalist parameters will be dealt with at some length in the next chapter, but first we need to examine the relationship between the information revolution and capitalism in a more general sense.

The central issue is whether technological changes, however profound, actually transform the manner in which economies are organized. To put it another way: is the information revolution incompatible with the continuation of modern capitalism? As regards advances in technology, in the first volume of *Capital* Marx argued that an organized industry under capitalism

> never looks upon and treats the existing form of a process as final. The technical basis of that industry is therefore revolutionary, while all earlier modes of production were essentially conservative. By means of machinery, chemical processes and other methods [modern industry] is continually causing changes not only in the technical basis of production but also in the functions of the labourer and in the social combinations of the labour-process. (Marx 1974a: 457)

For Marx, technological upheavals (however profound) in the production process did not immediately indicate a passage from capitalism, but rather were the way in which capitalism renewed itself. Unlike previous 'modes of production', capitalism includes within its normal operations the search for new processes and new technologies. The argument that the introduction of new technologies transforms the manner in which the economy is organized is not self-evident if we think of capitalism in these terms. The transformation of the technical means of production is what capitalism does continually.

Indeed, Karl Marx and Friedrich Engels famously argued in *The Communist Manifesto* that the bourgeoisie, whom they regarded as the agents of capitalism, retained their powerful position by constantly revolutionizing the (technological) means of production.

> Constant revolutionising of production, uninterrupted disturbance of all social conditions, everlasting uncertainty and agitation distinguish the bourgeois epoch from all earlier ones. All fixed, fast-frozen relations, with their train of ancient and venerable prejudices

and opinions are swept away, all new ones become antiquated before they can ossify. All that is solid melts into air. (Marx and Engels 1967: 83)

Although this was written before the more recent acceleration of modern capitalism, much of it sounds familiar. Marx and Engels invoke the continuous changes in technology that impact on society, and note that in the past social relations in the economy were governed by tradition and historical practice, but are now uncertain and thrown into disarray. (And what better characterization of the information age could you wish for than 'All that is solid melts into air'?) Again, taking this perspective, upheaval and disjuncture of social relations are the everyday stuff of capitalism, not signs of its obsolescence.

In the third volume of *Capital* Marx discusses the circulation of capital from money to commodity and back to capital again, which allows the extraction of surplus and therefore the accumulation of more capital. Each time (financial) capital is invested in production, which is then sold at more than it cost to produce, a surplus appears. This surplus (profit) adds to the original stock of capital; it enlarges the capitalist's stake, which can be reinvested. The faster this circulation (the more times in any given period an amount of capital can be used to produce commodities), the higher the possible overall capital accumulation. This leads him to note that the 'chief means of reducing the time of circulation is improved communications' (1974b: 71). While in this instance Marx was concerned with physical communication, roads, railways and shipping, this was due to the physicality of the products capitalism focused on at that time. In an age of information products, a similar relationship between informational products/services, the speed of communication and possibilities for capital accumulation can be observed. Thus the move to business models which have promised instantaneous ICT-mediated delivery of services or products is intended to radically shorten the cycle Marx observed, from laying out money for production (of goods or services) to getting it back in payment (with a profit). But even material goods' cycles can be shortened by the deployment of powerful ICTs. Dell Computer's customers configure their own product and directly feed their order (via the company's web-page) into the production programme. This speeds up delivery and thus payment (with its attendant surplus), making Dell one of the most profitable makers of personal computers in the world.

For Marx, therefore, technological advance is a key element in the reproduction of capital and thus in capitalism itself. But this should not be taken to indicate that Marx was a technological determinist; while identifying the role of technological advance in capitalism, he also emphasized the growth of markets, demographic shifts and other elements that had expanded effective demand and therefore supported the move to new forms of economic organization based on the accumulation of capital (Rosenberg 1982). Capitalism is a social system, not a response to technological advances, and it is to the general characteristics of this system that I now turn, to demonstrate their continuity in the information society.

Commodities, (information) capitalism and the division of labour

To put it most generally, for capitalism to exist there must be capital (as well as *capitalists*, the group who control capital in its various forms: finance, the actual means of production or land). Furthermore, capitalism revolves around the relation between property holders and those who have only their labour to bring to the market. If capitalists are to make a profit and therefore accumulate more capital, as they must do if they are to reproduce their capital, they must find things to buy and sell, and most importantly they must find things to buy which can be combined in various ways and then sold for more than their collective cost. This requires a regime of property rights to allow for the legally sanctioned transfer of resources (including labour) from one group to another. Historically capitalists have managed to render many things as property, and the expansion of intellectual property represents merely another phase in their need to mobilize raw materials (their inputs) as legalized property.

As a result, at the centre of Marx's analysis of capitalism was commodification: the appearance of relations between individuals as a relationship between things. The most important 'thing' to be rendered as a commodity was an individual's work, or labour. By depicting labour as a commodity, capitalism presents the appearance of an equal exchange in a neutral market (Marx 1974a: 77). For Marx, the labour process exhibited two characteristic phenomena:

> First the labourer works under the control of the capitalist to whom his labour belongs . . . Secondly, the product is the property of the capitalist and not that of the labourer, its immediate producer . . . The

labour process is a process between things that the capitalist has purchased, things that have become his property. The product of this process belongs, therefore, to him. (1974a: 180)

Furthermore, Marx crucially determined that the division of labour required a division between those who owned property in the means of production (whatever they were) and those who laboured with these means as workers (and who were paid accordingly). The distinction is between the owners of property and the owners of labour. Despite its formal appearance of (legalized) neutrality, there were power differences that were obscured by this commodification. Those who control capital and can therefore spend it on labour, on machines or even on consumption goods for themselves are in a better (more powerful) position than those who only have the (potentially commodified) labour they need to sell to earn the money to purchase the means of life (food, housing). While capital can be accumulated (and then stored for later use), labour cannot.

Importantly for Marx, the division of labour also relates to the divisions *within* the labour process, within work itself. Any specialization in industry reflects and reproduces the way tasks in general have become divided between people in society. And with this specialization of tasks, there are potentially new possibilities for setting up firms to deliver the products of these tasks (Marx 1974a: 333–4). In the historical development of capitalism this also has involved the commodification of knowledge and information, previously embedded within skilled processes, or as tacit knowledge. By dividing processes into specialized tasks, the holistic knowledge of whole processes is broken up by the division into simpler operations which can become the subject of less skilful repetitive labour. Equally, through specialization new industries and services have been developed from tasks that were previously embedded within more general processes. What were previously parts of complex operations reappear as subsectors of industries, or even new sectors altogether, and thus amenable to capitalistic organization and accumulation strategies.

This process has been furthered and accentuated through the development and deployment of ever more powerful technologies, and is 'completed in modern industry, which makes science a productive force distinct from labour and presses it into the service of capital' (Marx 1974a: 341). The use of technical and analytical knowledge ('science') is therefore not the novelty that Daniel Bell and others supposed. These innovations, alongside the demand for profits and new market opportunities that have characterized capitalism, are centred on the process of commodification: the rendering of 'things' and services previously delivered outside market relations as commodities produced by capitalists. Additionally, as new goods and services enter the market realm, they can be utilized by capitalists to produce (through combination) more new products and services. This move into the market is not a 'natural' occurrence. Capitalists actively seek new markets outside their locality to sell already developed products and services, or *within* their locality to bring into market relations currently 'under-provided' goods or non-market activities which might be turned into profitable activities or products. As the division of labour has become increasingly complex, more activities have been opened up for commodification. This can be best seen in the move of services from the social sphere of family provision to the market sphere where prices can be exacted and profits made.

The emergence of particular divisions of labour is not the natural act of benign history, but the result of power and control by capitalists over economic activities. The sorts of power which are mobilized in different sectors of the capitalist economy vary, though not as much as one might think. Nevertheless 'it is power constellations which shape the position of different knowledge experts in society, their immediate work situation, the development of specialization in their work, their relations to other occupations and the institutional protection of varied prerogatives' (Rueschemeyer 1986: 139). There may be advantages for the highly skilled, in that power over their working lives is diffused and negotiated, but as with any skill, the advantage gained is not fixed or unchallenged. Power over the value and prestige of the new knowledge-based occupations no more lies with the professions than it lay with the nineteenth-century weavers. The progressive division of labour into its constitutive tasks is driven by capital's need to produce more efficiently (through specialization), and it is capitalists' view of 'efficiency' which determines the particular division of labour at any specific point in time (Rueschemeyer 1986: 181). To be explicit, it is not technical efficiency itself that drives forward and structures the division of labour; rather it is those who are able to define 'efficiency' in particular ways who define, control and shift the division of labour.

Stephen Marglin suggests that one of the driving forces behind the long history of the development of the division of labour is the need for capitalists to hide their (unwarranted) appropriation of surplus by claiming that only they can organize complex processes (Marglin 1974: 38). This control of the workforce (through the division of labour and the limitation of holistic knowledge about the production and other processes) links back to the market for labour. Here labour is reduced to a service which can be bought in to deliver certain (possibly skilled) aspects of the production or service process at the behest of the employer. It is therefore unsurprising that Abigail Halcli and Frank Webster have concluded that in the (supposed) information society, 'most information workers are subordinate to the market place . . . The rise of informational labour appears to have done little if anything to limit the determining power of capital in the realm of work – or anywhere else for that matter' (2000: 74). Thus it is important to recognize that companies wish to define the knowledge of important workers not as the workers' skills and abilities, but as the (intellectual) property of the employer, like other elements of the means of production.

The intensification of capitalism, not its transformation

Capitalism has progressively deepened its penetration into previously non-commodified social relations. The recent moves to bring information and knowledge to the market as commodities, and the continuing commodification of tasks previously subsumed within more generalized practices as part of the division of labour are not unprecedented. Indeed, Ellen Wood regards the universalization and intensification of capitalist socioeconomic relations as the central tendency within capitalism. Like Marx, she emphasizes 'the logic of *capitalism*, not some particular technology or labour process but the logic of specific social property relations. There certainly have been constant technological changes and changes in market strategies. But these changes do not constitute a major epochal shift in capitalism's laws of motion' (Wood 1997: 550). What Wood calls universalization, 'the increasing imposition of capitalist imperatives, a capitalist "logic of process", on all aspects of life' (1997: 554), cannot be regarded as ushering in a new form of socioeconomic organization. Looking back at the history of modern capitalism, this 'logic' is always evident, but it is not an ahistorical logic, it does not exist outside (apart from) the history of capitalism itself.

Fernand Braudel's distinction between the economy (the market) and capitalism itself, between the 'economic life' and the activities of capitalism, underlines this point. Although this distinction is an analytical one only, as 'it is very difficult to draw a line indicating what . . . is the crucial distinction between capitalism and the economy', it is nonetheless useful (Braudel 1982: 455). For Braudel, a form of economy is operating 'when prices in the markets of a given area fluctuate in unison . . . [and] in this sense, there was a market economy well before the nineteenth and twentieth centuries' (1982: 226). An economy is a device, embedded within society, for the coordination of demand and supply which produces prices which enable exchange mediated by money of goods that have been socially produced. This contrasts with capitalism, which intervenes in the economy by producing goods or services specifically for profit, speculatively. The capitalist earns a socially recognized (and legitimated) return on investment (enabling capital to be reproduced and accumulated) when items are brought to market and successfully sold (Braudel 1982: 400ff.). Market economies can exist without capitalism and have done so, but capitalism cannot exist outside a market economy.

It is useful to make this separation of the notion of market from capitalism as it enables the analysis of changes in the form of market relations (most specifically the sorts of commodities and services brought to market) to be distinguished from the driving organizational logic of capitalists acting in the market itself. Thus changes in the social division of labour do not necessarily constitute epochal changes in economic organization. If we accept that markets are not the same as capitalism, then while they are interrelated, changes in the market's character do not indicate necessary changes in the 'laws of motion' of capitalism. The character of the economy may change due to technological or social changes, and this may expand or contract the possibilities for capitalistic intervention, but it does not change the reproductive cycles of capital itself. For instance, whatever initial claims were made for 'cyberspace' as a new arena for social interaction that would not be informed and structured by market relations, by 1997 Ronald Bettig could note that it was 'now most apparent that new computer mediated communications will be integrated into the existing communications system and serve primarily for selling commodities, including cultural goods and information' (1997: 151). Thus, while this might represent something of a change in the way the market itself appears, it by no means necessitates the end or transformation of capitalism.

There is therefore a clear distinction to be made between the forms of production under capitalism (the technologies or processes) and the continuing character of the relations of production. Technologies can change without any necessary corresponding shift in the way the economy is organized. Furthermore, the contemporary world is

> notable not for the dilution of 'economic' principles by a variety of extra-economic rationalities but rather for the degree to which political, technological and cultural 'logics' have been subsumed by the economic logic of commodification and profit maximisation . . . if there has been a major epochal shift since the 1970s, it is not a major discontinuity in capitalism but, on the contrary, capitalism itself reaching maturity. It may be that we are seeing the first real effects of capitalism as a comprehensive system. We are seeing the consequences of capitalism as a system not only without effective rivals but also with no real escape routes. (Wood 1997: 557–8)

This is to say that the contemporary period is not one where alternatives to capitalism have arisen (as the information society is sometimes presented), but one where capitalism itself has finally become the defining logic of the vast majority of the global system. Like Marx, Wood allows that there may be varieties of capitalism, from information societies to mineral exporting developing countries, but what is more important is the underlying common elements that all contemporary variants share. Capitalism is universalizing these common elements across the world, but as a system it is also intensified as more aspects of life are subsumed within the organizational logic of private property, commodification and profit.

The argument I have briefly set out in this section suggests that while the technologies and practices of capitalism in the market have changed in form, the underlying property relations – those between labour-owning and capital-owning groups – remain in substance unaltered. Although obscured through the presentation of new 'ideas' about economic organization, this represents a remarkable and crucial continuity, not evidence for a revolutionary new information age. Indeed, it is this continuity of the capitalist logic required for successful intervention in the economy that seems to be wilfully hidden by much of the discourse regarding the emergence of the information society and the 'new economy'. New technologies do not indicate a profound change in the underlying relations of production or their property-based organization. The nascent information society has already seen the expansion of the private rights accorded to information and knowledge owners rather than their evaporation (Boyle 1996; May 2000a). Information or knowledge may have an existence outside the privately owned realm, but this is increasingly a residual category, only recognized when all conceivable private rights have been established.

The economy of the information society is still driven by the need to earn a profit and for capital to be reproduced. To be specific, the relations between knowledge capitalists and knowledge workers remain essentially the same as between their predecessors under 'modern' capitalism. Capitalists control and deploy the knowledge outputs in a similar way to the products of their more materially oriented workers. This led Tessa Morris-Suziki to suggest:

> Information capitalism, therefore, not only exploits the labour of those directly employed by corporations, but also depends, more than any earlier form of economy, on the indirect exploitation of the labour of everyone involved in the maintenance, transmission and expansion of social knowledge: parents, teachers, journalists – in the end, everybody . . . the economic system itself becomes a vast mechanism for converting the knowledge created by society into a source of corporate profits. (1988: 81)

So while the methods of extraction may have changed, the logic remains unaltered. And although this may be shifting the forms of interaction, the use of non-commercial inputs (public services, parental socialization, unpaid housework) has historically been the unacknowledged support system capital has relied on to subsidize its labour inputs (Hodgson 1999: 124ff.). In the information society this reliance may have been expanded into new areas, but like Ellen Wood I do not regard this as a major shift: it is only an intensification of what has gone before.

The Informationalization of Society

The two sets of arguments which I have set out in this chapter lead me to conclude that in general, while much is changing, claims for an information age remain hyperbole rather than an acceptable characterization of contemporary society. The information society's technological shifts can be located in a continuing history of technology, while its economic organization is remarkably familiar. The history of technology and of capitalism indicates important continuities with the past. While there may be 'revolution' in ICTs, this has not brought about the wholesale social transformation that is often presented.

Indeed, for Lewis Mumford, (information) technology commences with human beings' own mental activities directed towards changing things. While technological history has been fixated on the fashioning of tools,

> the invention of language – a culmination of man's more elementary forms of expressing and transmitting meaning – was incomparably more important to further human development than the chipping of a mountain of hand-axes. . . . For only when knowledge and practice could be stored in symbolic forms and passed on by word of mouth from generation to generation was it possible to keep each fresh cultural acquisition from dissolving with the passing moment or the dying of a generation. Then, and then only, did the domestication of plants and animals become possible. (Mumford 1966a: 308)

The effort to develop the ability to speak, this early technology of communication, enabled the dissemination and storage of experience which could then be improved and built on. Perhaps this was the real information revolution: only then could material technologies be developed through the collection of experience and the organization of effort.

If we accept that new ICTs are having *some* effects on society, and nothing I have suggested above precludes such an assumption, there is no need to assume as well that these developments are recent in origin. Indeed, some writers have started to trace the origins of the information age back to at least the nineteenth century, if not before (Chandler and Cortada 2000; Levinson 1997; Winston 1998). This might lead us to agree with William Wolman and Anna Colamosca that it could be 'that by endowing libraries across the country, Andrew Carnegie created an earlier knowledge revolution in the United States whose scope at least matches that of the information revolution created by Bill Gates and his competitors' (1997: 75). And, looking further back, the informational chaos of the internet is strikingly similar to the problems encountered by readers in the sixteenth and seventeenth centuries who were frequently unable to establish the veracity of printed texts, because of problems of piracy and unauthorized (amended and edited) editions (Johns 1998: 171). By widening our perception of what information and communication technologies are, which is to say avoiding the contemporary fixation with computers, we can easily recognize a much longer process and by doing so dilute any remaining notion of its revolutionary character (where revolution is something sharp and short).

Even John Naisbitt allowed that ICTs 'did not bring about the new information society. It was already well underway by the late 1950s' (1984: 13). And, extending this horizon, Wilson Dizard noted that the

> so-called communications revolution is, in reality, a succession of three overlapping technological stages that have taken place during the past one hundred and fifty years. The first of these was the Wire Age (1844–1900), the second was the Wireless Age (1900–1970), and the third is the one we are now entering – the Integrated Grid Age, in which wire and wireless technology are brought together in powerful combinations which will form the structure of the future global information utility. (1982: 47)

This long time line is also supported by James Beniger, who suggested that the emergence of an information society was predicated on the 'control revolution', itself a response to the forces unleashed by the industrial revolution (Beniger 1986). At the centre of the 'control revolution' was the capacity for instantaneous feedback, allowing adjustment and an enhancement of material usage. This had an impact on labour, not least by changing the practices of work (requiring both more skill in adjusting processes), but also the capture of tacit knowledge through formalization and subsequent automation. Beniger makes explicit the links between such control systems and the rise of the information society, while stressing the roots of such developments in the nineteenth century. Recognizing the importance of the manipulation of information for the management of industrial organization and production, and focusing on the increasing ability of technology to allow the control of processes do not involve a claim that this is a contemporary phenomenon.

Finally, we should also note that the celebration of the possibilities of the internet as part of the new information age is hardly original. Before the internet, as Dizzard noted, there were earlier eras of new communications technologies. The claims made for these new technologies in the nineteenth century are again remarkably familiar. In a study which makes explicit the parallel developments of telegraphy and the internet, Tom Standage identifies some striking similarities in public response to both technologies. In both cases public reaction was 'a confused mixture of hype and scepticism' (Standage 1998: 194). As we would expect, remembering Mumford's analysis of competing technics, Victorians both celebrated the telegraph as a new mode of communication that would further democracy and social communication for the good of all (to bring about peace among nations), and also saw it as allowing new methods of control. Businesses could be centralized (control could be direct with less delegation to outlying plants), and governments could much more easily direct their armies (and their societies) through swift and authoritative communication. As Standage concludes:

> Today, we are repeatedly told that we are in the midst of a communications revolution. But the electric telegraph was, in many ways, far more disconcerting for the inhabitants of the time than today's advances are for us. If any generation has the right to claim that it bore the full bewildering, world-shrinking brunt of such a revolution, it is not us – it is our nineteenth-century forebears. (1998: 199–200)

The celebration of the information society, the celebration of the new age, is predicated on the novelty of today. However, this 'new age' is neither unprecedented nor necessarily as novel as is often presumed.

In this chapter I have engaged with the general claims that are implied by the proclamation of the arrival of the information society, showing why I am sceptical about them. Having examined the 'big picture', I now move to some more detailed discussion of changes that have been included as part of the characterization of this new age. The arguments I have outlined in this chapter echo through the rest of the book. In the following chapters I examine the assertions which stem from these general arguments and many of the criticisms I have already made will be substantiated by the discussions in the next three chapters. This chapter has laid out the skeleton of my argument and I shall now put some flesh on those bones. At this point, while I hope I have demonstrated why I feel the 'new age' arguments do not really hold up, there is still the possibility that the literature of the information society points to some profound changes in particular aspects of our lives. In the next three chapters I shall look at three subsets of this claim and suggest that even in this more limited sense, the assertions of revolutionary change are largely (though not completely) misplaced.

3

Information Capital, Property and Labour

Invocations of the information society and its 'new economy' are generally ambivalent towards the plight of labour, even though changes in the character of work are frequently at the centre of the observed (or proposed) transformations. Since Fritz Machlup and Marc Porat originally identified the prospective information society through an analysis of employment, the expansion of knowledge work or information-related labour has become an important indicator of the information society's arrival. Where these changes have been discussed at more length (in descriptions of the new society rather than merely as evidence of its arrival), the impact on workers is largely assumed to be beneficial. If there is some disruption, this is regarded as temporary and should not be seen as anything other than a cost of transition to the new age. But as William Martin notes: 'there is no aspect of the debate on the social impact of technology that has been more polarised between optimistic and pessimistic schools of thought' (1995: 119). Indeed, the few critical accounts have focused on the plight of (information) labour or workers, partly because they often originated with the left.

In mainstream comment on the information society, however, this lack of interest in the plight of labour means that when cyberspace (for instance) has been seen as a new forum for collective action, or a space for the renewal and construction of communities (as I explore in the next chapter), a discussion of class-based organization into groups oriented to labour, unions or work is frequently absent. Where inequalities have been recognized, they are more frequently regarded as between the 'info-rich' and the 'info-poor' (Haywood

1998), or between generations (Tapscott 1998; Negroponte 1995), than between the benefits which flow to capital and labour. One major reason for the lack of interest in the *real* plight of (informational) labour is that the notion of class has itself been the subject of considerable critique in the last twenty-five years (from the left and the right). Work in the information age is increasingly fragmented and the position of the individual worker so enhanced that for many the idea that there might be a collective interest by virtue of labour's relation to capital is regarded as outmoded.

The Transformation of Work

Analyses of the information society often assume that information work itself will transform labour. Information-based tasks are in ascendance and old-style manual jobs will be phased out through continuing automation. This argument usually involves reference to statistics showing how information workers are the fastest growing occupational group. Seldom did any author in the 1970s and 1980s manage to discuss the arrival of the information society without some account of the statistical material originally presented by Fritz Machlup and/or Marc Porat. Thus we find Daniel Bell utilizing figures drawn from Machlup's 'heroic effort to compute the proportion of GNP devoted to the production and distribution of knowledge' (Bell 1974: 212). Later, in *Megatrends*, John Naisbitt discussed Porat's findings under the subheading 'The information society is real' (1984: 20), while Tom Stonier asked: 'Porat may not be right but how wrong can he be?' (1983: 47). Indeed, Porat's is probably 'the best known – and certainly the most cited – study' of the emergence of the information society (Webster 1995: 11). On the basis of 'no smoke without fire', any shortcomings of Porat's (or Machlup's earlier) analysis disappeared under the sheer weight of statistical evidence.

This analysis is then linked with an identification of more flexible working practices enabling workers to use their expertise and skills in ways that allow greater job satisfaction. In this new world of information work, we are all empowered to develop our own job and profit from our own resources (our intellect). While recognizing that there may be some who will not benefit from the information revolution (in his example a fifty-year-old steelworker, chosen no doubt to emphasise previous *industrial* work), Nicholas Negroponte supposes the typical knowledge worker will be like Michael

Crichton, writer of bestselling books and screenplays, working at home producing knowledge wanted by others and thus able to profit from its sale or use (Negroponte 1995: 94). The claim for the transformation of work is therefore both quantitative (more and more work is becoming information work) and qualitative (information work is profoundly different from work in an industrial society).

The triumph of the 'creatives'

In the new era 'more and more of the economy's added value will be created by brain rather than brawn' (Tapscott 1996: 7). Unlike the 'old economy' where workers did not own the means of production, Don Tapscott suggests that in the new economy 'the means of production shifts to the brain of the producer' (1996: 48). The ability of individuals to work on their own behalf will be greatly enhanced, and many of the management practices of the past will be dissolved: close management is hopelessly inefficient in the information economy. Additionally Tapscott suggests that information and communication technologies (ICTs) have an inherently non-hierarchical character which points to a future of less stratified societies. In a world where 'most of the workforce becomes knowledge workers . . . [there will be] a profound democratization of corporate ownership' (Tapscott 1998: 232–3). Firms will be owned by their own workforces, and these firms' most valuable assets will be their worker/owners' intellectual resources. Furthermore, firms will contract out nearly all tasks, making Hollywood project-based employment typical of the new age (Gates 1996: 177; Lash and Urry 1994: 114–16). New ICTs will transform the relations of production of the economies in which they appear, promoting fluid networks rather than ossified hierarchies.

Knowledge workers are at the centre of many information society analyses, with commentators often agreeing with Charles Handy that the portfolio worker (Handy 1994: 175ff. and *passim*), charging fees rather than receiving a wage and working on successive time-limited projects, is the future of work. Negroponte also sees an expansion in self-employment: 'by the year 2020, the largest employer in the developed world will be the self' (1995: 237), dissolving the historic gap between the employed and the employee, between worker and boss. William Mitchell awoke one morning and 'discovered – as did many others – that I no longer had to go to work. Not that I suddenly became idle; it's just that work now came to me. I did not have to set out every morning for the mine (as generations of my forebears had done), the fields, the factory, or the office; I simply carried a lightweight laptop' (1995: 3). And with this realization Mitchell, like Charles Leadbeater (1999) and others, has recognized himself as belonging to the advance guard of the information society. In this new informationalized environment we, like them, can (re)construct our working lives rather than accept conditions employers thrust upon us. Collective bargaining (on a national or even a firm-by-firm basis) is a thing of the past. Knowledge workers choose how and when they work, control their own knowledge resources and therefore capitalize on their skills, while enjoying self-controlled work patterns negotiated to reflect their individual needs.

In her influential treatment of the impact of ICTs on the organization of work, Shoshana Zuboff suggests that these new ICTs will reduce the relevance of hierarchy and engender new, open and more cooperative ways of working (1988: 342ff.). Esther Dyson agrees, and suggests that this will remake the balance between labour and capital inasmuch as it will put the balance of power into the hands of the 'creatives'. They will be able to use the freedom to contract in the labour market to ensure their own satisfactory reward and level of working (Dyson 1997: 55–77). Like Handy, Leadbeater, Mitchell and others, Dyson presumes that most (if not all) work in the information society will be similar in its essentials to 'creative' work. Individuals, as intellectual/information workers, will have greater control over their work and thus greater satisfaction in its completion. But she also recognizes that some of us might prefer the more secure and stable working conditions of the postwar period.

Recently *The Economist* noted that resolving this tension between capital's desire for flexibility and labour's for security in the emerging information economy 'looks like being one of the great social, political and economic challenges of the next few decades' (Economist 2000a: 115). And as Richard Reeves of the Industrial Society has pointed out: 'While for some highly skilled workers the job-hopping mobility of the new labour market is exhilarating, for others simply staying in the race is unnerving' (2000b: 25). Nevertheless these changes will have to be accommodated rather than resisted, since change in the information society's labour market is inevitable. To 'stay in the race' many workers, from the information related to those delivering low-level services, are having to accept new, less secure conditions of employment.

For the optimists, this has two clear and important results for labour. First it allows greater leverage to the individual: now that the means of production are located in the mind, the significance of the threat to withdraw labour is enhanced. Knowledge and informational tasks are immediate, and employers are unable to store up output as a way of weathering industrial action or, more likely, unorganized casual absence. This should stimulate better working conditions and more 'enlightened' management to encourage loyalty and commitment to the employer, minimizing days lost. Conversely, as labour becomes more individualized, the 'free worker' may emerge, loyal only to themselves. Competition for the talented may become more important for companies than competition for customers (Caulkin 2000). Secondly, creative work is much more rewarding and less onerous than manual work. This is exaggerated by comparisons between working at manual/industrial, or even mining, jobs (often presented as Dickensian in character), and work in the offices of the professional classes. It would be difficult, nevertheless, to argue that information work was as *physically* tiring or as dangerous as manual employment. The advantages of informationalized (service) work (not least the possibility of sociability between provider and client) allow a positive comparison that carries much weight. But transferring from one sort of employment to the other is not necessarily easy.

Technological (un)employment

The recognition of technological unemployment or the disappearance of certain types of jobs due to automation or mechanization has been an integral part of the discussion of the social impact of the development of new technologies, from the plough to the internet. Information technologies are by no means the first machines to prompt concerns about technological unemployment. It is no wonder that, as John Naisbitt pointed out in the mid-1980s, 'computers have inspired fear and mystery in workers ever since their powers were first uncovered. Computer technology is to the information age what mechanisation was to the industrial revolution: it is a threat because it performs functions previously performed by workers' (1984: 29). Like farm labourers, weavers and people in any number of other jobs which have been overtaken by automation and the development of technology in the past, many have looked at computers in the last twenty or thirty years and seen their own jobs either devalued or scrapped as machines did them cheaper, quicker or more 'efficiently'.

Nevertheless, a recent report by the European Union's Information Society Project Office concluded: 'There is a justified consensus based on the experience of previous waves of technical changes that job losses should be more than compensated by new job creation' (IPSO 1998: 10). New technologies also bring new products and new services, which represent new employment opportunities for those whose jobs have disappeared. But some commentators have recognized that 'workers are not economic statistics whose lives can be measured in balanced-out equations . . . [the] shift is never smooth for the men and women involved' (Dizard 1982: 34–5). Although the transition between careers (and skills) may be painful, the problems associated with technological unemployment are still most often regarded as transitory and unavoidable. In the discussion of the information society and its economic relations, it is common to stress that it represents a return to individual *responsibility* as well as empowerment for labour.

Robert Reich (President Clinton's first Secretary of State for Labour) in *The Work of Nations* emphasized that income equality was closely related to the level of education (1991: 205). Therefore, in an age of knowledge work, low levels of education were likely to be reflected in low wages and the existence of the 'working poor'. His recommendations for the alleviation of poverty therefore focused on the improvement of individual capabilities: job-training programmes; childcare to enable single mothers more time to train; remedial education for the functionally illiterate; and an earlier start to education for the poor (with intensive preschool programmes) (Reich 1991: 249). But the blame for unemployment and underemployment was firmly placed on the individual, despite the changing structure of the global employment market. Reich divided up work into three broad categories: routine production services; in-person services; and symbolic-analytical services. Symbolic analytical services are expanding (these are the knowledge workers), and so are in-person services (delivered directly to the recipient), while routine production services in manufacturing are being automated where only low skills are required (or exported to locations with low labour costs) (Reich 1991: 174–8). Reich therefore recognized, more than many other commentators, that the sorts of non-manual work that would be part of the information society would not be exclusively for 'symbolic analysts' but would also encompass an expansion of in-person services.

The rise of services

Accounts of the effect of the deployment of ICTs on labour have focused on the character of the remaining work opportunities in the information society. As Diane Coyle notes, 'most jobs created during the past 20 years have been in the service industries, a wide category that covers everything from nursing to policing to working as an accountant or designing video games'(1997: 45). These forms of employment have figured in discussions of the information society since the early years. In the early 1980s, concluding the Club of Rome's broadly critical report on the impact of ICTs (Friedrichs and Schaff 1982). Adam Schaff (one its editors) suggested that automation through the deployment of ICTs *would* change the sorts of work done in much of society. However, this transformation would not be complete because society was unlikely to become fully automated in the foreseeable future, and therefore many tasks would remain for human employees.

Schaff identified five areas where employment opportunities would remain and even expand (areas we would now group together as 'services'):

1 'Creatives': for Schaff, ranging from research and development to fashion design. This is the group that more recent writers have regarded as paradigmatic of the new knowledge workers.
2 Organizational workers: Schaff argued that management, organization and other facilitative tasks (ranging from healthcare to entertainment) would still be delivered by people rather than machines.
3 Social workers, ranging from advisers through to what would now be called 'carers' of various sorts (and where we might now also include the self-development industries, from counsellors to aromatherapists).
4 Maintenance and technical staff, who will keep the machines running (from plumbers and engineers to the new support staff on the IT helpdesk):
5 Leisure activities, ranging from sports to cultural activities. Schaff linked this with an increase in leisure time through

automation, enhancing the time available for these activities (and the desire to do them better). (Schaff 1982: 341–2)

Thus while the report argued for government action to deal with the problems that would be likely to stem from the widespread changes in occupational structure from the deployment of ICTs, Schaff also saw considerable opportunities for (service sector) employment.

However, the service sector is not undifferentiated, nor necessarily uniformly embedded within the formal economy. More recently, writing on the information society has regarded the expansion of the social economy, or the 'third sector' as it is sometimes termed, as another key area of work. Whereas Schaff saw this as part of an overall continuity in employment (his group 3), the discussion of the third sector nowadays suggests that the information society will expand the organization of such tasks and activities outside the traditional public (state) sphere, or the market economy. Both Jeremy Rifkin (from a pessimistic and critical stance) and Diane Coyle (from a more positive position) suggest that future employment must involve the further development of a new sector of social services. For Rifkin, 'preparing for the decline of mass formal work in the market economy will require a fundamental restructuring of human participation in society' (1996: 273). And Diane Coyle argues that only by embracing the technologically driven changes in the economy and supporting the expansion of 'community, social and personal services' can the problems of mass unemployment be avoided (1997: 63–88). Methods for providing a 'social wage' will need to be developed for this new independent sector, which delivers many socially useful services to those in the two other sectors, but is predicated neither on public/state direct involvement, nor on undiluted market relations. Often represented by local organizations serving local needs outside the market, the third sector is often concerned with informational services, and even advocacy (and funded by donations and grants). The challenge of the information society is therefore to ensure that these new services provide a living for those involved in their delivery.

Even without this new sector, states such as America, Canada and Britain have undergone a large-scale shift to service provision. Manuel Castells suggests that these three states represent a new 'Service Economy Model' of economic development (1996: 228). The information society is most developed in these countries and has led to the expansion of services, and service sector employment.

Moreover, Castells concludes that despite considerable diversity in comparisons across countries outside this group, there is 'a common trend toward the increase of the relative weight of the most clearly informational occupations (managers, professionals and techni-cians) *as well as the overall "white collar" occupations (including sales and clerical workers)'* (1996: 218, emphasis added). Importantly for our purposes, it is generally argued that services involve a much greater level of information use and input than manufacturing tasks. This includes business services (services provided to other market actors – from advertising and legal services, to security, catering and clerical services), and the expanding sector of personal services (from counselling and training to babysitting, plumbing and gardening). By including all these sorts of jobs as services and then arguing that these services all involve the mobilization of infor-mation in one manner or another, it is relatively easy to see how the arrival of the information society can be substantiated.

The arguments made by Machlup and Porat over thirty years ago are still deployed to verify the emergence of the information society. Once the category of services is enlarged to include interpersonal services, from professional advice to personal trainers, it seems clear that the information-related sector of employment indicates a shift in the structure of society (if this is related to the employment profile of a society). These jobs are usually also regarded as more pleasant and more rewarding than those they replace, and thus the emer-gence of the information society has clear social benefits. However, if we examine these quantitative and qualitative arguments a little more carefully, they become rather less convincing.

Statistics and the Information Society

Taking the issue of quantitative change first, the use of various employment statistics is often presumed to firmly establish that the information society is emerging. The shifting balance between the posited category 'information work' and other occupations is sup-posed to indicate the extent of the transformation. This was the central element in the pioneering studies by Machlup and Porat, and has been repeated in subsequent treatments of the information society. However, this approach has two distinct shortcomings. The rate of expansion of information-related employment, as well as the threshold at which the information society might be said to have arrived, are difficult to determine. There is also the problem of

RARITAN VALLEY COMMUNITY COLLEGE
EVELYN S. FIELD LIBRARY

settling on a definition of information work which is *significantly* different from other sorts of employment, important if the information society is something new.

First, the threshold problem: the expansion of information employment has not been uniform nor continuous. Indeed, prior to any possible surge in the wake of the widespread use of the internet, it was reported that the expansion of the proportion of employment nominated as 'information-related' in the United States (utilizing the methodology of the Machlup and Porat studies) seemed to have largely halted after 1970 (Duff 2000: 58; Webster 1995: 13). In 1980 another study on information labour (again using Machlup and Porat's categories) found these occupations accounted for only around one-third of all employment (Duff 2000: 58). This was only about 6 per cent higher than Machlup's figure for 1958.

However, Herbert Dordick and Georgette Wang, using different measuring protocols (but ones they claimed were broadly compatible with Porat's), produced figures of over 53 per cent of the total US workforce in information occupations in 1980, rising to over 56 per cent in 1989 (Dordick and Wang 1993: 143). If over half the workforce is doing information work, the information society surely must have arrived, in America at least. On the face of it this could be regarded as a reasonable claim, but even if accepted, these figures reveal a considerable slowdown in the expansion of information work. Between 1970 and 1980 the share of information work increased from 39.2 per cent to 52.2 per cent, but increased by less than five more percentage points in the next decade. Furthermore, while these figures are initially quite convincing, cross-country comparisons suggest a problem. Using the same methodology, some middle-income states in Latin America and elsewhere had in the 1980s a similar level of information workers as the United States at the time of Machlup's study, but would hardly be regarded as approaching the widespread informationalization of 1960s America (Dordick and Wang 1993: 46–57). This leads Dordick and Wang to question the importance accorded to such figures, as they do not seem to capture what might be different about an advanced information society. While their analysis predates the surge in international internet use, it remains to be seen whether the more recent localized (and primarily urban) expansion in ICT usage in middle-ranking countries is the beginning of a more general informationalization.

Statistical analyses do not easily support the arguments that lie at the heart of the epochal claims of much commentary on the infor-

RARITAN VALLEY COMMUNITY COLLEGE
EVELYN S. FIELD LIBRARY

mation society. An extended period when little expansion of information-related employment can be identified in the society most often regarded as leading ICT-related developments suggests claims for the dawning of a new age might be a little premature. Furthermore, as the above suggests, without an agreed definition of 'information-related work', figures can vary quite widely. And this is the crux of the problem: it has proved difficult to find a definition of information employment that is both satisfactory and reveals the changes which would need to be found to substantiate claims for the arrival of the information society. Often, to get round this problem, increasing levels of information-related work are taken as synonymous with (the more easily measured) shift to a larger service sector. But this is not an accurate reflection of the varieties of tasks which lie below such broad generalizations, nor does it firmly support the claim that we have entered the information age.

While informational jobs (from 'symbolic analysts' to all manner of 'professions') may be increasing, these are very different from jobs which involve the delivery of personal services to clients (based on the skills and knowledge of individuals). These latter services are not traded internationally or even transregionally, but rather represent localized economic relations (from hairdressers and plumbers, to garden designers and personal trainers). These jobs are much less revolutionary than the examples often presented as typical of the information age, but represent a larger segment of the employed population, especially if transport and distribution services are included (Islam 2000). Indeed, as Schaff pointed out twenty years ago, these types of service represent a marked continuity with previous modes of employment.

In any case, the identification of an increasingly professional workforce has been achieved through a statistical sleight of hand. Only by accepting that the renaming of employees with more professional-sounding titles is evidence of an actual functional change, as well as supposing all those involved in the putative knowledge sector *are* professionals or high-level knowledge workers, could a claim for a substantive change in employment patterns be supported (Kumar 1995: 25–6). This is not a robust proposition. Taking the 'creatives' as paradigmatic of the new workers, around 1 million workers in Britain might be regarded as belonging to this broad group (Glaister 1998). However, this is less than 5 per cent of the workforce, and even adding professionals (and other business services), this is not a proportion of the working population which can be taken as broadly typical. Where these workers have support staff, from secretaries and assistants to security and cleaning staff, a claim that all of these are also information workers stretches credulity.

Furthermore, the statistical expansion of service occupations can be 'explained in terms of burgeoning social and technical divisions of labour throughout the industrial system' (Sayer and Walker 1992: 104). The emerging knowledge and information industries are seldom the result of completely new types of enterprise or product, but are more often the result of the continuing division of tasks into their constituent elements. This results in important statistical anomalies. Although manufacturing is reported to account for only 20 per cent of contemporary British domestic product, a recent study by the Warwick Manufacturing Group for the Engineering Employers Federation suggested that this figure understates the share of output by nearly a third. The real level of manufacturing's share of gross output was nearer 28 per cent of domestic product (Morgan 2000). This is mainly because many services are actually services *to* the manufacturing sector (whose employment and output statistics used to include these workers and products before they were spun off or outsourced). These services remain part of the process that produces *material* goods, even if the particular knowledge service sector itself does not deliver materialized outputs. These may be recoded as service jobs, but they have merely been transferred from large (and vertically integrated) corporations to smaller scale suppliers of 'outsourced' services. Once the share of the state is also removed from these statistics (although many tasks carried out by the state are clearly informational and have been for some time), the 'expanding' service sector accounts for only around one-quarter of economic activity in Britain.

The forms of the division of labour may be new, tasks may emerge and be subdivided or aggregated with the aid of new technologies, but the changes this produces are more statistical than real. In any case, as Ursula Huws has pointed out, the focus on new service occupations is misleading: 'the growth in service employment over the course of the century can only be demonstrated convincingly by leaving out domestic servants, whose numbers have declined steadily as employment in other forms of service work has risen' (1999: 33). Once service employment is taken to *include* domestic servants, the shift to service employment, identified as characteristic of the information society, is much less dramatic. Indeed, the problems of defining information work as different seem insurmountable when looked at in a wider historical context:

when did most workers *not* use information and knowledge of some sort? Such problems with this method of identifying the emerging information society prompt Alistair Duff to dismiss all statistically based accounts as 'inherently dubious' (2000: 19–68, 150). The difficulty of defining satisfactorily the information sector(s) renders such claims difficult to sustain at anything more than a very general level.

Turning the information society argument on its head, Duff points out that even if we accept that current advanced societies *are* information societies, it is actually rather difficult to show that other societies are *not* (echoing Dordick and Wang's international comparison). 'The general point is that it is very difficult to prove . . . that modern societies are more information-based than other societies. There is something *prima facie* suspect, perhaps even arrogant, about the assertion that *we* are now, while *they* were not then, living in information societies' (Duff 2000: 171–2). This brings us back to the argument in the previous chapter regarding the claim for revolution. If we allow that information tasks are important and widespread, then it is difficult to argue that this is a recent development and that the information society is radically different from other societies. If we suggest that information work is broadly coterminous with the service sector, then this does such violence to the notion of information work as to make it an almost meaningless category. When we look at work in the service sector the claims for the transformation wrought by ICTs seem rather hollow.

What is Service Work?

Whatever the changes in the character of the workforce in various countries (and the problems of capturing these changes statistically), the consensus is that the service sectors (widely understood) in states such as America, Canada and Britain have expanded considerably relative to manufacturing and agricultural activities. But, although it is often claimed that the 'new economy' is service driven, few contemporary commentators seem aware of the diverse character of services. Service occupations range from knowledge-workers to cleaners, but in Leadbeater's view, for instance, it is empowered knowledge-working individuals who are typical. He fails to recognize the very different experiences of those offering high-level professional services and other service 'providers' (Leadbeater 1999: 63–4 and *passim*). For Leadbeater and others, jobs in the information society are by definition more rewarding, and so can only benefit the workforce relative to their previous employment. This problem of misperception stems in the first instance from an uncritical acceptance of the evidence of quantitative shifts (discussed above), but also from an apparent ignorance of what service workers actually do.

While an uncritical assertion that computerization leads to comprehensive deskilling is misleading (C. Smith and P. Thompson 1998: 554–6), the opposite argument, that all work in the information society is highly skilled, is no more convincing. Much information-age work is routine service work which may be quite lightly managed and reasonably flexible. But it is not necessarily particularly satisfying on a day-to-day basis. One recent study suggests that there is likely to be a growing distinction between the increasingly complex knowledge required to provide some sorts of services (which will therefore retain the levels of satisfaction previously enjoyed by high-level service providers) and the tendency for other tasks to be reduced to a series of standardized practices. Here, high labour turnover, atomization of the workforce and 'dumbing down' are likely to be evident (Frenkel et al. 1999: 273). This division between a highly skilled element and deskilled functionaries has frequently been the product of automation and is not a recent development linked to the information society.

Much service sector employment is related to sales in one way or another. This work is often perceived as more satisfying and autonomous than office work: 'sales people experience work in much the way small business owners do – as a challenge . . . [but] in bad times, or in periods of increasing competition, salespeople experience their work as stressful' (Frenkel et al. 1999: 268). However, these workers use ICTs only incidentally; instead they use their personalities as their key tools. And as databases and automated (expert) systems are increasingly deployed, personality will become more important. A salesperson's complex communicative and social skills will become relatively more valuable to the employer than their store of (tacit) knowledge.

When, for instance, the Midland Bank (now part of HSBC) set up a stand-alone telephone banking operation, run from a single-site call centre,

First Direct explicitly trie[d] to avoid recruiting bankers to call centre and sales positions, feeling that different skills and attitudes [were] required. There are still banking staff in important areas of the busi-

ness but, where possible, First Direct tries to systematise functions
which were previously judged to require banking skills, for example,
risk assessment. The main determinants in staff selection are behav-
ioural skills, personality characteristics, and specific abilities such as
phone manner and ability to work as part of a team. (Richardson
1994: 322)

Other banks, such as NatWest (Stanworth 1998: 58), have swiftly
adopted similar practices, as have other service providers using call
centres (Taylor 1998). Work-based skills have been replaced by managerial perceptions of social skills. This enhances the power of those
who decide whether the worker 'has what it takes'; there are no
'objective' criteria for social skills that can be appealed to in disputes or dismissals, only subjective assessments (coloured by personal values and prejudices).

The move to personality as 'value added' for the employer is a
continuation of a trend that predates the posited emergence of the
information society. In a prescient section of his classic study, *White
Collar*, C. Wright Mills discussed the postwar emergence of a 'personality market'. The personality of the salesperson became commodified because it produced value for the employer by increasing
sales and could therefore be regarded as part of the contracted
labour purchased in the work relationship (Mills 1953: 182–8). These
skills have become of wider import as more workers become service
providers and has been referred to as 'emotional labour', the need
to enact particular personality types on behalf of the employer (Belt,
Richardson and Webster 2000; Hochschild 1983; Taylor 1998). One
of the key effects of the widening use of ICTs may therefore be to
heighten the value of people. A recent report on the effects of ICTs
on the workplace, reported in *The Economist*, concluded: 'Front-
office workers with "people skills" and good managers (in the old-
fashioned sense of that term) are the main winners from the IT
revolution' (Economist 1999a). Interpersonal interaction is the new
key skill for many jobs. But given the subjective element in judgements in this area, the power held over employees may become
more arbitrary and less subject to negotiation.

At the other end of the spectrum, knowledge workers (or
'creatives') often enjoy considerable latitude in their work practices
and have complex work patterns. But their work is also demanding and stressful, and perhaps most importantly very competitive,
'so that social relations are less satisfying than suggested by the
image of the empowered work organization' (Frenkel et al. 1999:

270). Thus this development may not be quite as positive as it is often presented:

> If anyone has become a portfolio person it is more likely that he or she is a conscript of organisational restructuring than a new breed of entrepreneur. Becoming the victims of downsizing, subcontracting, outsourcing, contingent contracts and other forms of organisational restructuring is not a situation favoured by most, and given the opportunity such workers – manual, non-manual and managerial – would happily return to the ranks of full-time permanent employment. (Warhurst and Thompson 1998: 20)

Not only do the statistics mislead, but the fragmentation of the division of labour to produce these new knowledge workers has been forced. While some have clearly benefited from these shifts and continue to do so, the use of ICTs in the workplace reflects the organizational practices of the employer rather than any 'natural' tendency of the technology. And, therefore, in the service sector it is likely that work practices will be designed for the convenience and benefit of employers, indicating something less than a wonderful new world of work.

The issue of power disparities between the employer and the employed remains central whatever the claims for flattening hierarchies and devolved management. As Will Hutton pointed out:

> Edwardian England employed millions of maids; millennial England employs millions of child-minders and personal-fitness trainers. The insecurity and dependency on the rich faced by both is no less real . . . Income inequality is not a fact of nature produced by the weightless economy; there is a power struggle to capture added value which cannot be wished away. (Hutton 1998)

The service tasks where extensive employment growth is taking place are those provided locally, not the high-level knowledge services presented as typical of the information society. The rise of what many in America regard as 'McJobs', as well as the expansion in numbers of cleaners, builders and others working in the 'shadow economy', is part of the 'new economy', not something it replaces.

At the heart of the information society, in California, the divergence between those in the favoured jobs and those who work in insecure, casual service jobs has been characteristic of the labour force for decades. In a regional economy which has always 'benefited' from the low-cost labour of (illegal) immigrants from Mexico and elsewhere, the divergence of possibilities in the information society is readily apparent. For instance, rising property prices have pushed many homes further and further from the sites of service jobs; while software programmers and other high-level information-related workers reside near their work, those who service them (from police, to teachers, from gardeners to waiters) are condemned to two-hour commuter journeys and low incomes (Vulliamy 2000). These problems also effect such hot-spots of the 'new economy' as Cambridge in Britain. Furthermore, while the richest fifth of workers in Silicon Valley saw their real average income rise by 19 per cent, that of the poorest fifth fell by 8 per cent between 1991 and 1997 (Economist 2000a: 115). Although there has been some organized resistance, most notably among California's janitors in spring 2000, insecure jobs and illegal status have limited the ability of unions to organize this workforce.

The increase of service employment does not necessarily indicate that all service jobs will be either pleasant or secure: quite the contrary. If we divide information work into two ideal types (however difficult this might be in practice), originating work and processing work (Huws 1999: 42–3), only the former is likely to be an improvement in terms of working conditions, and even this is far from certain. Many jobs may involve both sorts of mental activity, but the jobs which feature heavily in many accounts of the information society are those which emphasize the originating aspect of knowledge and information-related tasks. But if we examine all those services and jobs that need to be included to produce an argument that most of us are involved in information work of one sort or another, it is the latter category of processing tasks, along with much more precarious personal services, that dominate. And these tasks are far from the world of symbolic analysts and portfolio workers.

The End of Work as We Know It?

The theme of this chapter echoes Richard Walker's statement: 'Mostly forgotten in present-day paeans to high-tech and high skill, of information age and "symbolic analysts" are the great swaths of ordinary jobs held by ordinary people' (Walker 1999: 269). For those workers who generally process information rather than originate it there are few advantages to the information age, and substantial costs relative to the stability of the full-time, permanent work that was on offer to many (but not all) after the Second World War.

Increasingly that period of full employment looks as if it was less a new settlement and more an anomalous period in terms of labour relations (Esping-Andersen 1999). In many ways the postwar bargain between capital and labour (as regards employment relations, at least) is unravelling in the information society.

Some extreme pessimists have argued that work for many will slowly but surely evaporate. George Spencer claims that humans will increasingly become completely irrelevant to the processes of the production of goods and the delivery of services. The numbers excluded from society because they lack any saleable skills will expand because the information revolution, unlike earlier technological advances, 'will not create a demand for new forms of labour, for it will perform an increasing proportion of all activities itself' (Spencer 1996: 75). No organization will retain human labour once cheap and quick computing can duplicate the task. The system will be more efficient but reduce large segments of the population to poverty. Whereas previous technological unemployment has been largely self-correcting, information technology precludes this process repeating itself because ICTs automate tasks faster than new jobs can emerge (Spencer 1996: 62). This 'end of work' thesis has been popularized by Jeremy Rifkin (1996) and received considerable attention in recent years, but it is rather overstated. Work itself is likely to continue, but its character is changing and in this sense the 'end of work' is the end of certain forms of work. Disputes have centred on whether this is an advance for labour or not.

Unhealthy trends

The reduction of hierarchical power, regarded as symptomatic of the use of ICTs in the workplace of the information society, has been balanced by a move towards contract, term-limited and casualized labour rather than the wholesale displacement of work itself. Power and authority have been reimposed through the terms of employment typical of knowledge work. Insecure employment is reconceptualized as an opportunity for individuals to bargain for the maximum reward from their employers through individual contracts. For instance, at Microsoft's headquarters nearly a third of the workforce are 'permatemps'. They are employed through agencies, and lack the stock options, health insurance, pensions or paid holidays of their more favoured colleagues. Indeed, in recent disputes about the conditions of employment for these workers, Microsoft denied they employed them at all, asserting that they merely contracted work to them as service providers (Borger 2000b; Klein 2001: 249–52). These sorts of contractors are often referred to (using Handy's phrase) as 'portfolio workers', moving from one job to another, delivering focused labour and building a portfolio of experience which is reflected in their (supposedly) high rewards. But in this case, such a description disguises the ability to hold workers at arm's length to minimize the employer's responsibility to them.

The portfolio-working knowledge worker is often based at home, but not all homework is knowledge work or even information based. Across the world, much of 'women's unregulated work is home based' (Prügl 1996: 42). This ranges from tasks approximating to information-related work (telephone operators working from home as in the British directory enquiries network) to the traditional networks of textile homeworkers that can still be found in areas of Britain (such as the East Midlands) and elsewhere. Piece-workers for electronic manufacturers in Silicon Valley are also often home-based: like much of the valley's low-wage labour, they may be illegal immigrants scraping together a living and avoiding detection by the police. Homeworkers of all types account for around 10 per cent of the UK workforce (TUC 1998: 12), and a higher proportion of service workers. For the favoured, a portfolio career is an opportunity to work from home on different projects in varying teams; for the rest it is the hell of balancing multiple low-paid part-time jobs. And for many small-scale service providers, acting as 'sole traders' or self-employed, their home environments provide few of the technical, support and other facilities that employees in large organizations take for granted.

Home-based workers suffer from many problems their full-time, company-employed colleagues avoid: zero-hours contracts (where no hours are guaranteed and staff are used on-demand); no paid 'comfort breaks'; no paid holidays or sick days; and they are seldom fully covered by health and safety regulations. Even when they work for only one employer, home-working service workers are usually regarded as self-employed and paid by results. In the service sector, the 'evidence is that these workers have become freelance ... not because of the attraction of self-employment, but because of cost-cutting through downsizing amongst employers and the increased use of outsourcing' (Stanworth 1998: 57).

Additionally, the health effects can be serious. Summarizing her research for the Department of Health on the use of ICTs by home-based workers (teleworkers), Barbara Steward notes:

> The constant presence of work to the worker, the coterminous boundary of work and home and their ability to work despite symptoms encouraged non-recognition, or containment, of illness . . . the health and happiness of telework employees became the personal responsibility of individuals, absolving employers of their accountability for health and safety. These effects often encourage them to work longer into illness, during illness and/or return sooner in convalescence (Steward 2000).

Full-time homeworking intensifies the work process, ensuring that the employer extracts the maximum amount of labour from the employee, and allowing no real health-related pauses for recovery *within* the paid working day. Homeworkers, even high-level knowledge workers, often 'feel guilty for being at home – so they end up working longer' (Cary Cooper, cited in MacErlean 1999). In the main, the experience of information piece-work (data entry, data coding, directory enquiries) in 'electronic cottages' is far from the knowledge workers of the information age literature.

The key aspect of contract working, whether it be homework or project-based work at a company's main site, is that it distances the employee from the employer legally and socially. While it is in the interests of employers to invest (and promote the well-being) of a permanent workforce, these interests are diluted by contract work. If a worker is ill, another contractor can replace them. This is the fear that many homeworkers and contracted staff regularly live with. If particular projects need particular skills, why invest in training when a 'portfolio' worker can be contracted to do the job. In this sense the individualization of the workforce in the information society enables companies to retreat from responsibilities for their workforces that were fought for throughout the twentieth century. It is the individual's responsibility to train themselves, to invest in their skills, and this is a view with widespread political currency. This shift of responsibility is often presented as a means by which workers are able to use their individual skills to obtain a better bargain in the labour market, but the reality is very different. Companies, with a choice of workers and with large reserves of cash, can bargain much harder than can individual contractors needing to meet their regular living costs. But even when an information job has been secured, there are other problems.

Command, control and surveillance

Information and feedback has always been used to control the processes of work. The recognition of its crucial importance, alongside the development of new methods of information use, was a central element in the 'second industrial revolution' at the end of the nineteenth century. Indeed, Peter Drucker has suggested that the introduction of scientific management (or Taylorism) was 'the most important step toward the "knowledge economy" . . . The key to producing more was to "work smarter". The key to productivity was knowledge, not sweat' (1968: 271). Although there were a number of problems with the asserted 'scientific' bases of the system (Noble 1979: 273–4), the utilization of high levels of information about work practices to aid the control of the workplace became a key aspect of management in the twentieth century and shows no sign of receding in the new millennium. Certainly, information, surveillance and efficiency, 'the very principles of Taylorism [have] become intensified, extended and automated through the application of new communications and information technologies' (Webster and Robins 1989: 339). Scientific management has been enhanced by the information revolution, not rendered obsolete. Furthermore, the use of ICTs limits choice in working practices through the need to work with already supplied, complex software which channels both effort and output. Despite the seemingly more powerful and 'open' nature of these tools, they set quite limited parameters to the possible methods of much information-related work (for instance, through scripted responses in call centres, or the limited range of selectable responses in credit-scoring software).

Taking the example of call centres (possibly the paradigmatic information workplaces), workers are subject to high levels of surveillance (Fernie 1998). While this is hardly unprecedented, and often represents a revival of practices which many thought (or hoped) had been dispensed with, ICTs have greatly enhanced the ability for workplace surveillance. This should not be overstated, however: opportunities remain for workplace resistance, and even if these are constrained they should not be automatically discounted (Bain and Taylor 2000). Furthermore, due to the direct access employees now have to many of the important information resources of the company, resistance includes (as it always has) direct sabotage. Research in America for the FBI concluded that over three-quarters of attacks on computer systems were actually carried out by disgruntled employees (Hilpern 2000b). Surveillance through ICTs is increasingly commonplace, because the technology itself has been developed in a manner that eases information retrieval regarding performance, yet this has not halted these attacks.

It has enabled increasing oversight of email, however. This has raised further questions regarding the rights of employees to privacy, but also the rights of employers to ensure messages sent out from their systems are legal, decent and do not compromise their business (Gillies 2000). The ability to (surreptitiously) monitor and oversee work practices conflicts with the right to privacy workers enjoy under Article 8 of the European Convention on Human Rights (IER 2000: 15). Nevertheless, in a recent discussion of surveillance and privacy at work, Michael Ford suggested that it was likely that surveillance was more widespread than ever before. This was partly due to the use of ICTs, which have 'removed many of the economic obstacles to constant surveillance' (Ford 1998: 10). This may not be only to the advantage of the employer: in Zuboff's study of the impact of ICTs on the organization of work, workers she interviewed in the mid-1980s hoped that the enhanced ability to provide 'objective' management information (throughout the firm's systems) might make victimization over performance and accuracy/skill issues more unlikely (Zuboff 1988: 342ff.). But equally, the awareness of oversight encourages self-monitoring and control; labour has nowhere to hide and workers must presume that they may be monitored at any time (Zuboff 1988: 323). And it is this sort of effect which has been much more evident than the provision of 'objective' information through which work disputes could be settled, although the processes of supervision through surveillance are never comprehensive or uncontested.

Regardless, the use of ICTs in the service workplace enables the manager and/or employer to monitor and control their workers more extensively and less obviously than previously. While in itself this may act as a suitable encouragement for self-discipline, even more insidiously, surveillance has moved beyond the immediate confines of direct work practices. The increasing ability to retrieve information through data-mining, access to computerized records and information-market operations, as well as the development of new data forms (new tests, for instance), has led to problems regarding the privacy of workers. Employers increasingly are intercepting emails and in some recent cases have sacked employees circulating (or merely receiving) 'inappropriate' messages (Arlidge 2001;

Inman 2000). Pornography has been the chief concern of employers, but in a bid to stamp out racist and sexist jokes, emails containing such material have also resulted in sackings. And it is not just low-level staff who have been disciplined; in one law firm lawyers who circulated an email regarding oral sex between colleagues have been suspended. Human rights issues have been effectively sidelined because of the subject matter of the messages, despite their clearly private nature.

In Britain at least, the Data Protection Act 1998 goes some way to reinforcing the rights of individuals to prevent the disclosure of aspects of their private lives. But information regarding the use of alcohol and other drugs (through mandatory workplace urine testing), as well as health information, has all been enhanced through the deployment of various (though not necessarily information) technologies. Off-duty behaviour is increasingly monitored by employers and may result in demands for cessation or dismissal (Hilpern 2000a). There is software available which its makers claim can detect alcohol and drug (ab)use by analysing patterns of absence from work (Gillies 1999). Any protection afforded by the law may be rendered ineffective by a consent defence, where employers claim the information on which judgements were made was submitted voluntarily by staff. Courts seldom enquire how free such consent may have been (consent to information under the duress of job loss is seldom regarded as coerced) (Ford 1998: 26). In this, the wider aspect of the information age is revealed.

While ICTs may allow better record keeping and searching, new tests and new types of information of relevance to the management of the workplace have been 'discovered'. The manager's right to manage is invoked to defend the increasing amounts of data required by the employer and these can all be used to build up complex pictures of workers which are then fed into the monitoring process. From psychological testing to routine appraisal meetings, the information-gathering processes of management often seem relentless. If 'knowledge is power', in this case it represents the power of the employer over the employee. But although management through the control of information may be enhanced in the information age, it remains a continuity with previous practice not a novelty.

The ability to control and monitor through the deployment and use of ICTs has enhanced the ability of managers to manage their workers, and continues previous modes of employment by new means. The move to more contract work (including portfolio working) brings back a labour market that resembles the early history of capitalism (short-term contracting, putting out, few workers' rights, and periodic lay-offs). This represents a dilution of the postwar compromise regarding the relations between labour and capital. But these continuities of control and the reassertion of individualized labour relations have taken place alongside another significant (and more general) continuity with previous modes of economic organization.

The Continuity of Property Relations

Having suggested that the transformation in the workforce overall seems unconvincing and that, for many, the issue of control in the workplace remains central to their experience of work, I now turn to the continuity in class relations. Taking class in its Marxian sense, which is to say the distinction between capital (the owners of the means of production) and labour (those who have only their own exertions to bring to market), the obsolescence of class in the information age is greatly exaggerated. Despite claims that we now live in a 'classless' society, the information society remains divided by the ownership of (intellectual) property. As I argued in the last chapter, there is a serious problem with concentrating on new technologies at the expense of the social relations in which they appear. Who owns and who does not own intellectual property tells us much about the 'new' information society.

One of the key aspects of the information revolution has been the largely successful attempt by capitalists to remake the information economy in the shape of the previously existing material goods economy. Specifically this has been accomplished through the utilization and legitimization of property in knowledge: intellectual property rights (May 2000a). In the information society, the recognition of the importance (and value) of knowledge and information resources has reinforced the desire and need of capitalists to control, own and profit from such resources. Similarly to the way in which the landowning aristocracy, during the growth of intensive farming, sought to enclose what had previously been common land, intellectual property is predicated on the remaking of knowledge and information as property despite its potential free availability. The rendering of knowledge as property through patents, copyrights, trademarks and other instruments transforms knowledge that might be regarded as commonly available to everyone into property owned by the few. (In the appendix I outline the forms of intellectual property and the ways in which property in knowledge is usually justified; here I discuss the effects of making knowledge and information property in the workplace.)

By controlling the resources needed for knowledge work, through the patenting of particular processes or technical procedures, capitalists maintain their ownership of the means of production. If companies control aspects of the information and knowledge required for information-related work through patents and copyrights, individual contractors are forced into a relationship with these owners, rather than enjoying the forthright independent existence posited by Handy or Leadbeater. Where new resources are developed, employers aim to capture these from the worker and enclose them for themselves. From Taylorism's codification of tacit shopfloor knowledge, to the development of software today, employers have always wished to control and 'own' the knowledge developed by their employees and contractors.

Valuable information or knowledge cannot be left to the free flow of ideas, often regarded as characteristic of the information age. Companies need to stop such flows, and as John Kay points out in his advice to managers seeking the *Foundations of Corporate Success*,

> if the company is to add value, it needs to create organisational knowledge from the skills of its members. This is achieved when the combined skills of two experts increases the value of each. The problems the organisation faces are, first, those of securing the exchange of knowledge and, secondly, those of *preventing that knowledge, and the rewards associated with it, being captured by one or both of the individuals concerned.* (1993: 73, emphasis added)

This exploitation of the production of knowledge and the prevention of capture by the employee is not something that might typify a new epoch; rather it represents a continuity with the social relations (between labour and capital) of modern capitalism.

In the information age, therefore, there is still an important distinction between the property-owning class and those who work for them. While intellectual property is justified on the basis of the recognition of individual creativity, in the real world (rather than the imagined world of legal philosophy) there are considerable barriers to individuals profiting from the ideas and knowledge they originate. On one side companies ensure that in most employment (and service) contracts any ideas which come to the knowledge worker, either during their working day or (perhaps more importantly) due to the task they have performed for their employer, are rendered the property of the employer (May 2000a: 119–24). This is the first method of capture. To ensure these ideas are not taken to another employer, employment contracts include an almost ubiquitous non-disclosure clause. The second method of capture is slightly different: especially with artistic creations (which are subject to copyright), the costs of reproduction and distribution are beyond the means of most individual creators (not least of all, academic authors). Thus publishers, record companies and other distributors of cultural creations can request the effective transfer of the intellectual property to them in return for bringing these creations to a wider audience. While the internet has facilitated some specialist (self-)publication, Stephen King's attempt to side-step the (mass) publishers by direct e-publication recently failed due to the difficulty of policing free-riders (Waters and Grimes 2000). At least publishers provide a mechanism for ensuring that authors receive *some* reward.

This is echoed by the defensive use of the patent system by large corporations who either buy out those inventors who have managed to patent an idea, or rely on the increasing expense of the process of filing a patent to ensure that inventors find it hard to garner any protection for their innovations. James Dyson, for instance, was forced to abandon one of the elements of his complex of vacuum cleaner patents because he was unable to afford a renewal fee when he was still trying to start production – it is now being used by his competitors. Although lawyers argue that the payment for renewal is to ensure that the patent is being worked while it is protected, the fees remain trifling for large companies but onerous for individuals wishing to protect their invention while trying to market it (Halstead 1997). Even if the inventor takes out a patent, the struggle is not finished. Unless they are able to form their own company to take advantage of their invention, they need to interest a backer or manufacturer. Dyson Appliances, which remains independent, is an exception: an inventor's own successful firm. More often desperate inventors at the end of their funds accept an unfavourable licensing agreement from a manufacturer and lose much of the eventual benefit from their inventions.

Indeed the battle to own particular intellectual property is seldom won by the individual worker or knowledge creator, and losing can often be costly in the extreme. While not typical, the example of Petr Taborsky is instructive (Perelman 1998: 83; Shulman 1999: 106–12). Taborsky was a talented undergraduate college student in chemistry and biology, who worked as a laboratory assistant at the University of South Florida College of Engineering in 1997. He was employed to study methods of making sewage treatment cheaper and more efficient. After the project had ended Taborsky claims he developed a reusable sewage cleanser, a compound similar to cat litter, which was potentially a major innovation in sewage technology. And this is where Taborsky's troubles started. The project he had worked on was sponsored by Florida Progress, a utility holding company which owned the rights to all the research outputs. Though Taborsky claimed that his reusable cleaner was developed separately from the research project he had worked on, a jury found in favour of Florida Progress, accepting their argument that he could not have developed this idea *unless* he had worked on it during the project: therefore the new technology or product was owned by them as the project's sponsors.

Taborsky was subsequently convicted of also stealing university property (his own notebooks, used to work through his ideas), leading to a sentence of three and half years imprisonment. Due to the particularities of Florida law, Taborsky started his sentence on the chain gang. He was swiftly removed from it after a public uproar in respect of hard labour for an intellectual crime. On the other hand, he did himself few favours in this case, not least of all by signing agreements regarding the ownership of research materials with the university and Florida Progress, which he then broke. Whatever the intricacies of the case, one thing is clear: no one doubts that Taborsky made the discovery. However, by filing for patents on these discoveries, he made the ownership of the ideas the key contested issue. While the optimists of the information age might assume that an innovation belonged to the innovator, in the real world of contracted research, of expensive research equipment and any number of other impediments to truly independent discovery, Taborsky and other 'creatives' are essentially 'brains for hire', not self-owning innovating minds.

While the Taborsky case is clearly an extreme example (with complex circumstances I have skated over here), Seth Shulman compiled an entire book from similar sorts of battles regarding ownership of intellectual property (Shulman 1999), and my own book on intellectual property details a number of other cases (May 2000a). Additionally, as Kenneth Arrow noted in 1996, there is continuous litigation about the mobility of technical personnel; previous employers are trying to put obstacles in the way of future employment which would in any way use skills and knowledge acquired while working for them . . . we are just beginning to face the contradictions between the systems of private property and of information acquisition and dissemination. (1996: 127)

In the intervening five years, these issues have attracted ever widening attention from employers and lawyers. What matters here is that the laws of intellectual property may seem largely to be directed at the protection of the rights of the individual, but this is seldom the case outside legal textbooks. Rather, intellectual property allows the separation of the individual from the products of their own mind, reproducing the alienation of the worker from the product of their labour which was central to Karl Marx's characterization of capitalism. As intellectual property is (legal) property, its effects are similar. While the internet has prompted significant problems regarding digital copying and transmission, which has many copyright-based industries (like the music industry and Hollywood) very worried, in the workplace intellectual property relations largely continue to ensure that the knowledge worker's output belongs not to them but to their employers.

The information society's characteristic property relations are therefore little different from those of the previous (industrial) society, although the sorts of work carried out by the low-skilled may be a little more pleasant (while many personal and social services remain largely unchanged). The information age is less benign and empowering to labour than many have presumed, or promised. The white collar worker, as well as the portfolio working, flexible professional on contract or project-based employment, no longer enjoys the security of their predecessors. Much effort has gone into giving this a positive spin, but it all looks less empowering when work is scarce and bills need to be paid. As Reeves points out, while 'Leadbeater and [his] ilk can take some time out, then land another plum job, for the average British worker a spell out of work means a 10 per cent pay cut if they get another job' (Reeves 2000a). And where jobs become 'low-wage, part-time and temporary (and non-union) [this] amounts to a massive distribution of income from labour to capital' (Sayer and Walker 1992: 103). But this is not the only possible threat to the well-being, wealth and employability of labour in the information society's leading countries.

(Information) Labour in the Global Economy

At the centre of a number of proclamations about the possibilities of knowledge work in the information age, there is also a somewhat doubtful implicit claim about the intellectual advantage of the advanced economies. It is not self-evident that the developed countries have any natural advantage when it comes to intellectual activity. A number of quite high-level tasks (such as software development) are already conducted by workers in countries outside the core information societies. Furthermore, tendencies in international trade and investment 'point to a much more open world in which differences in labour costs . . . are becoming increasingly transparent and are likely to lead to relocation pressure. Not surprisingly, that pressure is likely to be greatest for high value-added commodities which have low unit transport costs – often new, high-technology commodities' (Freeman, Soete and Efendioglu 1995: 601). Those tasks that can be delivered from a distance will be opened up to competition from lower cost locations, and it is wrong to assume that these workers are unable to perform information-related tasks – they clearly can. But merely the possibility of relocation is beneficial to employers. For instance, in unionization disputes in America, Kate Bronfenbrenner found that despite threats, few plants were actually moved. Employers merely used the perceived plausibility of easy relocation as a bargaining lever against workers' demands (Bronfenbrenner 2000: 52). The promotion of the information society has introduced such bargaining logic into new areas, to the benefit of employers of information workers in developed states.

Additionally, and worryingly for those depending on information work to save the economies of America, Canada and Britain from growing unemployment, the increasing international (and potentially global) character of the information services market is already leading to real price competition for some services (most especially routine, backroom, information-processing tasks). India, a number of Caribbean countries and some cheap labour areas of Europe are already competing for the very service tasks which the 'Service Economy Model' of economic development policy relies on to re-employ those affected by technological unemployment (May 2000b; Wilson 1998). Where information-related work becomes mobile and partially deskilled through the deployment of ICTs, there is little reason to suppose that it will still be carried out in relatively high-wage economies. Information-related service tasks will become subject to the same pressures that have affected manufacturing employment for many years. As in textile working, electronic assembly or shipbuilding, the labour market for information work will become increasingly global, leading many jobs to be moved to where they can be most cheaply undertaken. Not all information jobs will migrate (just as not all manufacturing jobs have done), but many will be subject to (implied) global price comparisons, in the same way as the jobs of the Midlands' textile workers and Scottish metalworkers have been.

While this represents a comparative opportunity for some countries and regions to provide information services, the case of the Indian software industry illustrates the important advantages to employers. Although

> India's comparative advantage consists of a skilled English-speaking workforce that earns from one-fourth to one-eighth the salary of its East Asian, American and European counterparts . . . the 'relatively low wages' given to software personnel by multinational corporations are actually staggeringly high in Indian terms and in terms of local purchasing power. (Prasad 1998: 435)

The companies making use of these off-shore services are able to capture more of the surplus produced by labour by finding locations where competent and ICT-adept labour is cheaper. The advantages are not just savings in labour costs: in much the same way that call centres have avoided previous bank employees, so software multinationals have remade their work arrangements for their new workers (Prasad 1998: 441), dispensing with previous hard-won concessions.

The competition may also come from closer to home: Finland, home to the mobile phone success story Nokia, grasped the possibilities of the global information economy as a way of delivering itself from the recessionary early 1990s, remaking itself as a high-tech hub (Shaw 2000). And Ireland has also adopted this strategy, adding a tax regime that is extremely high-tech friendly (of which more in chapter 5). Thus, paradoxically, personal services (which are seldom traded internationally, or even at any distance domestically, and are hardly highly skilled in the sense of 'knowledge work') are likely to be the jobs that are safest at the centre of the information society.

High-level information and knowledge work may also be relatively safe, provided its practitioners are able to maintain the scarcity of the knowledge they mobilize, through professionalization and lobbying for regulatory requirements in their favour. But even here automation is starting to transform the skill composition of particular professions, most directly lawyers. In much the same way that opticians saw their oligopoly demolished by open price competition, the advent (at least for corporate services in America) of an online auction service has driven down prices for certain generic legal services (Trapp 2000). Online auctions for many other professions and services will no doubt have similar effects, as will websites that offer resources for basic and standard legal services. One service, Desktoplawyer.co.uk, claims that it is already handling 6 per cent of uncontested British divorces. And while many lawyers may object, Ronald Dworkin for one suggests that these services do not 'strike me as more dangerous than many lawyers' (quoted in Hobsbawm 2000). Once buyers realize that these services *are* standardized, price competition is likely only to increase, and though it is difficult to work up much sympathy for lawyers, other professions and service providers are likely to experience similar downward pressure on their fees.

The optimistic assumptions about the move to information tasks for those able to retrain therefore seem unlikely to be fulfilled. Indeed, the overall prognosis for information labour does not seem too good, especially when compared to the vision of a new age and a new world of empowered workers. Tied up with much that I have discussed in this chapter is a particular irony, perhaps best summed up by Stanley Aronowitz and William DiFazio: 'Just as large amounts of clerical labour were displaced by computerization and by devices such as the answering machine and the personal computer, a significant quantity of managerial labour can now be displaced by the computer's capacity to do the work of coordination' (1996: 67). Those who have sought to displace workers through automation and computerization have themselves, in their turn, found themselves on the firing line. In his particularly dystopian view of the information age, Ian Angell argues that there will be an elite of knowledge workers and a mass of service employees, but draws a different conclusion. The answer is to make sure that you are one of the 'new barbarians' who can take advantage of these factors, who can thrive and prosper in the new hyper-individualized information age, and who need to fight off the lower orders (Angell 2000: 228). Where others have seen the information age as an essentially progressive transformation, for Angell it is an enormous (though unavoidable) threat to the advances of the Enlightenment. Indeed, for Angell, it is not in the workplace that the greatest transformation of the information age will appear, but rather in the realm of politics. And it is to this issue that I turn in the next chapter.

4

Communities, Individuals and Politics in the Information Society

Having criticized some of the assertions of economic transformation in the last chapter, I now turn to the claim that information and communication technologies (ICTs) will profoundly alter political life. This usually involves the idea that the information society will allow greater political participation by individuals, facilitated by the enlarged potential for communication. Alongside this move to a more interactive politics, the state is presented as a political organization much too large and inflexible to respond to contemporary politics. New political communities counter (and challenge) the state's remaining political functions and role in society. The 'Californian ideology', the radical combination of hippie individualism and libertarianism that informs much of the debate about the information society, is virulently anti-state: the state is an oppressor rather than a facilitator of citizenship or welfare (Barbrook and Cameron 1996). I look at the role of the state in the information age in the next chapter, but first I examine the impact of the information society on individuals as political actors.

The market as coordinator of individual choices is taken as the model for political action in the Californian ideology. Individuals are not determined by class, race or gender, but rather make informed individual choices. The information society reflects Thomas Jefferson's ideal of a democracy: forged in response to the aristocratic and paternalistic views of enlightened rule developed by the Federalists, Jefferson's view of democracy instead stressed individual sovereignty and rights, as well as reduction of the role of government. Many have argued that the internet establishes a realm where 'Jefferson's fundamental democratic value – "free communication among the people, which has ever been justly deemed the only effectual guardian of every other right" – reigns without interference' (Post 1996). This is allied to an 'unquestioning acceptance of the liberal ideal of the self-sufficient individual', which owes much (in America at least) to the history of the frontier and the American revolution, fought against the oppressive laws and unjust taxes of the British Crown (Barbrook and Cameron 1996: 56). The internet's improved communications therefore allow individuals to communicate freely without constriction, promoting this form of democracy.

It is sometimes asserted that 'democracy is everywhere approved, though its true meaning is almost nowhere understood' (Hanson 1989: 69), but in the information age the Californian ideology has provided a clear and widely used 'Jeffersonian' definition. Here is not the place to explore the diverse meanings of democracy, but one central aspect is useful for understanding developments in the information society. Politics is dominated by the attempts by various groups (and individuals) to secure and further their interest in their freedom and liberty. Isaiah Berlin famously suggested that there are two dimensions to this interest: negative and positive liberty (Berlin 1997). Whereas negative liberty is the freedom *from* constraint, positive liberty is the freedom *to* achieve certain prescribed ends. The writings of the information society celebrants seem most often concerned with negative liberty, freedom from government and from constraint. While social democracy has historically been concerned with positive liberty, the freedom *to* achieve certain things (education and welfare, for instance), in the information society this seems less important to many than securing freedom *from* interference. There is a growing suspicion that arguments for positive liberties illegitimately encroach on negative liberties, on the right to non-interference while attending to one's (legitimate) interests.

Politics in the Information Age

Writing as the idea of information society started to attain a wider currency in the early 1980s, Wilson Dizard regarded 'information politics' as merely another forum for politics as it was already conducted (1982: 117–47). It would be a continuation of the interest group politics which had previously typified the American political process. However, politics would be 'given new force by the sophisticated use of communications in ways that often seem to favour direct self-serving actions over the more difficult, slower processes of consensus' (1982: 191). The trend towards political individualization has subsequently become an important element in discussions of information politics, and was almost immediately taken up by John Naisbitt. He argued that the information age enhanced an already clear move to decentralization and local politics: 'we are giving up the grand, top-down strategies, imposed from above, and substituting bottom-up approaches, that is limited, individual solutions that grow naturally out of a particular set of circumstances.' And because 'political power is decentralised, you can make a difference locally' (Naisbitt 1984: 102, 129). This theme remains popular: Charles Leadbeater recently argued that the information society encouraged the 'use of information and communication technologies to realise the utopian goal of self-governance' (Leadbeater 1999: 224). The linking of 'self-governance' and the information society is an often repeated refrain.

Twenty years ago in Japan, Yoneji Masuda presumed the information society would lead to a heightened interest in political participation because the 'technical difficulties that until now have made it impossible for large numbers of citizens to participate in policy making have now been solved' (1990: 83). As there are no longer practical barriers to fuller citizen involvement, the information age can move society towards a more participatory democracy. More recently, Don Tapscott reaffirmed that the information society's deployment of ICTs would lead to a 'truer democracy' because 'democracy is about choice, being able to make choices that determine the future' and ICTs greatly enhance the availability of the information and means to make such choices (1996: 309). The reduction of the costs of participation and the widening availability of the (information) resources to support such participation indicate an improvement in democratic deliberation. The furtherance of democracy becomes the removal of obstacles to communication.

The widening use of ICTs enhances and empowers individuals and groups through the expansion of possibilities for utilizing informational resources (and knowledge) previously hoarded by specialists and governments. In some accounts this allows the interaction between state and citizen to become reciprocal; interaction can be used to inform and shape the role of the state in civil society. But in addition the ease of communication will engender a surge of participation and initiatives in civil society, separate from governmental initiatives or those of state agencies. Jan van Dijk points out that this relies on people using ICTs to 'shape a politics of their own and bypass the government's co-ordinating role' (van Dijk 1999: 84). Nevertheless, it is assumed that new online (information) communities can be organized more swiftly and with a more widely dispersed membership than previous communities. And while previously it would have taken considerable resources to mobilize such groups, on the internet many of the costs have evaporated at the same time as communication has accelerated (Dyson 1997: 47). These new communities have become emblematic of politics in the information age.

Starting from the premise that technology 'has its most profound effect when it alters the ways in which people come together and communicate', Peter Kollock and Marc Smith see the (re)construction of community as one of the most important effects of ICTs on social interaction. These new communities 'meet any reasonable definition of community . . . they are not a pale, artificial substitute for more traditional forms of community' (Smith and Kollock 1999: 4, 9, 16–17). Indeed, they offer an improvement in the communicative and organizational potential of community. This leads Manuel Castells to identify a number of social movements which have built on these new possibilities: environmentalism, feminism and organized resistance to globalization (left-wing and right-wing). These emerging politicized communities, while originally organized on the basis of resistance to global capitalist society, are attempting to build positive bases as previous communal projects did. But the 'new power lies in the codes of information and in the images of representation around which societies organize their institutions, and people build their lives, and decide their behaviour. The sites of this power are people's minds' (Castells 1997a: 359). Community in the information age is elective; we join because we wish to, because we believe. This contrasts with more traditional communities we might belong to because of our class, our race, or where we live and work.

These new and different political communities build on democratic technics, free from centralizing authority. Indeed, for some, the internet is enabling the emergence of a potential 'cybercommunism' (Barbrook 2000). In the online gift economy, information and knowledge spread round the 'net' without cost: a new field of social relations has opened up which will supersede capitalism by undermining the centrality of property relations. Paradoxically, it is Americans who are pioneering this new communism, who have engineered a space outside capitalist social relations. Individuals get what they need, rather than only what they can afford, when information is given as a gift and not exchanged as a commodity.

New forms of political collectivity have emerged, from interest groups to mutual aid networks, all empowered to communicate through the use of ICTs, all benefiting from new modes of information and knowledge generation. But in tension with these communities there is also a move to greater individualism, empowered through information use, using ICTs to find the knowledge that will enhance lives. Here the information age ushers in the free individual, who can make the most of himself or herself, whose political participation is elective and driven by self-interest. In the information society we are all individual nodes in a vast social network, coming together in different patterns for different reasons. Therefore, though many writers discuss the possibility of new communities, there is also a supposition that each of us will belong to a number of different groups none of which we might take as finally defining our political identity. In this sense a proliferation of collectivities may coexist with rampant individualism. Whether this enhances democracy remains to be seen, but many of these changes are by no means revolutionary.

(New) Political Communities

Discussing the problems of identifying and according weight to new electronically mediated communities Craig Calhoun suggests that

> the excitement of the new technology may lead us to ask the wrong question, or at least proceed one-sidedly. Research projects commonly start with computer-mediated communication and then look for community ... But perhaps we should start the other way around. Look first for communities and then study the role of computers and other media of communication within them. (1998: 380)

If we do so, Calhoun argues, we would find that, while many communities have a presence on the internet, to call them 'virtual communities' obscures elements that are shared with their predecessors. While ICTs may engender more communication, they usually support networks which have been developed through physical meetings (at conferences, on marches, at events). Generally, communities involve exchanges built on social solidarity; they are diverse and continuing, consolidating complex and reciprocal contacts, while instilling in the members a form of collective responsibility for the upkeep of community and its shared norms. Although electronic communication may enhance these processes, 'the internet matters much more as a supplement to face-to-face community organisation and movement activity than as a substitute for it' (Calhoun 1998: 382). New ICTs may enhance already existing networks, but this is not the same as stimulating the development of new types of community.

Certainly political groups have used the internet to bring considerable national and international pressure to bear on governments in various struggles and disputes. The most widely cited example of political action across the internet is probably the Zapatista rebellion in Chiapas, Mexico. Although it is their supporters, not the guerrillas themselves, who make extensive use of ICTs, 'the Zapatistas have begun to craft their missives and adapt their public interventions as they have better understood the effectiveness of the internet in making their voices heard, communicating with supporters and forging new alliances' (Cleaver 1998: 629). By utilizing the internet, the Zapatistas' supporters have been able to organize a continuing series of large-scale protests and meetings, which have supported the rebellion and have encouraged the authorities to take it more seriously. This is taken as decisive proof that new internet-based political campaigns will transform politics in the information age.

But the Chiapas uprising also highlights some problems with this form of political participation and engagement. Due to the ease of copying or reproduction, a seemingly vast quantity of diverse information and knowledge may all stem from one or two initial sources, and may be less reliable than it at first appears. As Judith Hellman points out, while Harry Cleaver may be a responsible and committed activist for the Zapatista cause, it is

> astonishing that there is so little awareness that most of what we read about Chiapas, and civil society in general in Mexico, has been selected and transmitted by Harry Cleaver or a couple of other people whose political outlook – other than a passionate belief in the power of the internet and its potential to build a 'civil society in cyberspace' – is completely unknown to most. (Hellman 1999: 177, footnote deleted)

It is frequently difficult to assess the authenticity of information reproduced through the use of ICTs (not just the internet but also high-quality desktop published leaflets, for instance). Those most adept at using the technology may enhance their influence, while others who might have alternative information to offer can often lack the ability to fully deploy the relevant technologies, or even gain access to them.

Neither is it clear that information age political networks can mobilize effective campaigns. The success of the Zapatistas has largely stemmed from their physical control of territory in Mexico, not the internet campaign. In another widely heralded 'victory', the campaign against the Multilateral Agreement on Investment was largely organized (and took place) on the internet, and included the crucial (and decisive) leaking of a text of the draft document. But while ICTs enabled a faster dissemination of the text, aiding political mobilization and requiring the negotiators to release an 'official' text, the campaign was a passive recipient of a document leaked by one of the governmental teams, reflecting their own negotiating interests, not necessarily those of the campaign. More importantly, the negotiations finally floundered on the French delegation's realization that their 'cultural exception' would be rendered illegal, opening up French culture (particularly the cinema) to an English-speaking invasion. Thus internal problems played a decisive role in halting the negotiations, even if the internet-mediated campaign provided unhelpful publicity for the negotiating governments. Another high-profile campaign using ICT-based networks, against the North American Free Trade Agreement, was also conspicuous by its failure. And despite widespread demonstrations, the failure of trade talks in Seattle was again largely because of internal negotiating problems rather than a direct response to the protests.

However, these demonstrations against recent Group of Seven meetings and other international forums, such as the 'battle in Seattle' against the World Trade Organization (WTO), have garnered considerable public attention. And significantly, all were coordinated across the internet and mobile phone networks. Likewise, in Britain, Reclaim-the-Streets linked with other groups to create day-long demonstrations in the City of London in June 1999 and again in May 2000, while simultaneously demonstrations on the same anti-capitalist theme sprang up in other cities (Klein 2001: 311ff.). Networked and fluid organization makes it difficult for police to gauge appropriate action, or even where intervention might be required. Other campaigns, such as the September 2000 fuel tax protests by hauliers and farmers, have also been organized through mobile phone communications to allow a controlling group to remain dispersed and difficult to track. In Britain this use of ICTs (specifically mobile phones) first emerged during the 'summers of love' (1988 and 1989) when illegal rave party organizers played a complex game of cat and mouse with the police while trying (often successfully) to organize large-scale raves in peripheral countryside areas around London (Garratt 1998). Having noted the success of these operations, oppositional groups have adopted a similar strategy of 'just-in-time' demonstrations and political gatherings.

The (in)sufficiency of access

We are told that the new information politics will encourage more people to be involved with politics, because it will be easier to participate. However, standardization and use of expert systems has often decreased the ability of individuals to use their discretion at work, and Langdon Winner suggests that this is likely to produce a lack of interest in political activities as well, because of an assumption that similar limitations will operate in the political realm (Winner 1995). It should be no surprise if the decline in democratic participation is not reversed. The problem is not the ability to communicate, but is rather an issue of political will among the governed and the governing (van Dijk 1999: 235). What divides optimists from sceptics is the issue of the sufficiency of access and whether this alone will stimulate renewed political engagement.

Scepticism regarding enhanced democracy in the information age is not the preserve of the academy or the powerless. A recent report from the OECD stressed that there is a

> temptation to believe the information revolution is by its nature profoundly democratic. This belief also accompanied a number of other social and technological revolutions in the past – the introduction of printing, universal publicly funded education, radio, television and even the introduction of air travel. While these changes undoubtedly contributed to the evolution of democracy over the centuries, none, in and of itself, was a driving or determining force for positive change. (OECD 1998: 9)

Another report, from the National Working Party on Social Inclusion in the Information Society (partly funded by IBM) argued that although political communities might benefit from increased communications, '"being on-line" is not the same as being "connected" to a community of others (whoever or wherever they happen to be) who share one's interests. Getting on-line to the information highway is after all *only one stage – albeit a technically complex one – towards participation in and contribution to such a community'* (IBM 1997: 19, emphasis added). As these reports underline, we should always be wary of claims that the introduction of a new technology *automatically* produces a change in the political practices of society.

Democracy will still require an engaged community, albeit patterned to some extent by wealth and access to social and technical modes of communication. It will exclude those who are 'outside the loop' through the language used, the knowledge presumed, or the interactive practices maintained. This exclusion is not merely based on technical abilities; for many, the time commitment of engaging in politics is onerous. While people may be happy to vote in local or national elections, or even mobilize on the basis of certain issues, the idea of people committing more and more time to electronically mediated participatory democracy assumes that because the means are there everyone wants to expand their political involvement.

However, 'even if ICTs cannot overcome widespread apathy, they might well nurture those who are interested in politics and facilitate their deeper involvement' (Dutton 1999: 180). The deployment of ICTs may not have the effect on participation the optimists expect. As Bruce Bimber succinctly suggests, 'the Net will not alter the fact that most people are highly selective in their attention to political issues and their assimilation of information; they tend to care relatively intensely about a few issues while remaining disinterested and uninformed about most' (Bimber 1998: 155). The use of ICTs may help those already engaged in politics, who are already actively participating in democratic forums, but may not necessarily *encourage* engagement by those not already taking part. Certainly in Joseph Zelwietro's study of the use of the internet by environmental groups, those who were using email and other ICTs regarded them as *supplementary* to their other communicative activities, not their central arena of participation in the 'struggle' (Zelwietro 1998). The networks may be better connected but they remain essentially the same networks.

It is hardly surprising therefore that in one of the few studies of *actual* political activism on the internet, Kevin Hill and John Hughes concluded that those whose political activities have involved increasing use of the internet are a self-selected group of the already politically committed. Internet activists 'are probably not converted from typical citizens to political junkies but are more likely to be political junkies to begin with' (Hill and Hughes 1998: 42–4, 72). From right-wing militias and religious fundamentalists to the anarchist left, groups who have found other avenues closed to them (or at least unsympathetic to their messages) have migrated to the internet more swiftly (Bimber 1998: 156). But Alan Scott and John Street concluded that while these sorts of groups have 'added to the repertoire of political gestures and devices' they might use, they are adopting political practices which have emerged more gradually in the realm of the mass media. Politicized groups and communities still 'operate in instrumental ways to promote their interests as organisations' even if they now use ICTs to achieve this end (Scott and Street 2000: 234–5). The technologies may be novel but the methods have been imported from previous successful media campaigns.

That said, some localized deployments of ICTs to widen political debate have been (at least partially) successful. In Santa Monica, California, the Public Electronic Network (PEN) established in 1989 maintains a network of public access booths. Although it still tends only to reach the already politically active, these have included a wider variation of socioeconomic groups than indicated by ownership of personal computers. Most importantly it gave a space for the homeless to find an effective political voice in a mostly affluent community which was not attuned to their needs (Schalken 2000: 154–68; Schmitz 1997: 87ff.). But in many ways PEN is a space for discussion not advocacy, and by not taking votes or polls the network remained a *part* of existing political networks in Santa Monica rather than their replacement (Raab et al. 1996: 291). There have also been experiments in Minnesota and Toronto, as well as in Manchester, Grimethorpe and others sites around the UK (Day and Harris 1997). Often these 'electronic village halls' have garnered quite strong initial interest but have struggled to maintain it. Having in most cases been event led (either as part of local elections or campaigns about specific issues), once the initial focus has been lost they have failed to become ongoing forums. In some cases they have been captured by specific groups pushing a certain viewpoint, and mostly, despite the promise of increased interaction, local and national governments have taken little notice of the prescriptions emerging from such deliberation.

More often governments have used ICTs to make services more 'efficient' (Internal Revenue Services in America and Britain are moving to online submission of tax returns, for instance). Considerable attention has been paid to the manner in which governments can enhance service delivery through the deployment of ICTs (see, for instance, Taylor et al. 1996; Margetts 1999; NAO 1999) and governments themselves have emphasized this aspect of communication (White Paper 1999) rather than the democratic potential of ICTs. I will discuss the more general use of ICTs by governments in the next chapter, but the clear intent in Britain and elsewhere has been to enhance the management of information rather than profoundly change the way politics itself is conducted or to encourage an expansion of participation. The possibility of a transformation of political practices is seldom evident in the proclamations of ministers responsible for the informationalization of government. The new politics is pitched at the level of managerialism rather than an enhancement of political participation.

Especially while access remains less than universal, politicians can easily dismiss the results of electronic polling as unrepresentative, not least because of the self-selected character of the polled pool. And even when names are actively collected to support a particular campaign, the technology may count against them: 'nobody pays any attention to electronic petitions because they are so easy to fake electronically. "Non-virtual" protest costs time and money, and that's the point. As always, you get what you pay for' (Kohn 1999). Even if electronic state–citizen mediation becomes possible and widespread, perhaps Marek Kohn is right, it will never replace the weight of old-style campaigns of mass mobilization. Additionally, it may be less effective at generating petitions than actually asking people face-to-face. While Jubilee 2000 collected 150,000 signatures through its website to present to the Group of Seven (G7) leaders meeting in Cologne in June 1999, this was 'dwarfed by the two million collected in Peru alone, where most people don't have access to a computer, let alone the net' (Denny 1999a). Mobilization is about political will, not just access: proactive signature gatherers may well fare better than passive online signing. More bluntly, as the *Economist* noted of the primaries in the US presidential election of 2000, 'the people who have made the biggest fuss about the internet have all got one thing in common: they're the losers' (Economist 2000c). Effective political mobilization and interactivity may not be the same thing.

Information politics will not swiftly replace the previous modes of interaction and activity on the basis merely of the potential opened up by access to ICT-mediated networks. Issue-based politics may be enhanced by the flows of information available to activists and other interested parties, but to a large extent politics has always been constructed around issues, from food riots to machine breaking, from women's votes to nuclear disarmament. A change in political will is more important than a change in the technologies of communication.

A new political society?

The literature on the information society identifies two directions in which political communities might develop. As I have noted, there is an expectation of widening participation, with new communities emerging while older (established) groups enhance their activities. But conversely, an increasingly disengaged polity reduces the committed base which any political community needs to tap into to survive. As Marc Smith found, in a large-scale exercise to map 'the social structure of the Usenet', the 'most popular newsgroups, where the most people contribute messages, focus on topics related to Usenet itself, employment opportunities, and aspects of personal computer use', with political issues hardly figuring at all (Smith 1999: 204). It is a mistake, common among the politically active, to think that everyone is as interested in politics as they are. But the fear of a fragmented and individualized polity does seem plausible if political practices on Usenet are indicative: 'It tends to draw people into isolated groups, conversing among themselves' (Hill and Hughes 1998: 74). If people self-select their involvement and stick with groups they broadly already agree with, then the discussions which are central to democratic deliberation will be rendered more difficult, not easier.

When political debates *do* take place, the forms of interaction may preclude informed discussion. Short staccato statements exchanged at speed are not conducive to reasoned or extended discussion of complex issues (Hill and Hughes 1998: 109–31). Even Howard Rheingold, doyen of the info-democrats, admits that it is 'amazing how the ambiguity of words in the absence of body language inevitably leads to online misunderstandings' (1996: 427). This is not a recipe for sophisticated political discussion. Clifford Stoll points out that 'online debates of tough issues are often polarized by messages taking extreme positions. It's a great medium for trivia and hobbies, but not the place for reasoned, reflective judgement. Surprisingly often, discussions degenerate into acrimony, insults and flames' (1995: 32). This suggests that the internet as the proto-typical political space of the information society has yet to develop into an arena for political debate. While it may be possible to work through issues where most of those connected agree, leading to the refinement and 'improvement' of particular positions, this is hardly the same as a political realm in which political disagreements can be aired and possibly resolved.

The ability to move from one realm to another, to seek out those you agree with, may actually enhance the ghettoization of political opinion. This is in many ways a retrogressive move; rather than stimulating engagement and communication it may reinforce par-tisanship, antagonism and intolerance. For instance, in the online actions to resist the clipper chip (an encryption device with the key held by a state agency to ensure continued access to private, scram-bled, communications) and the MarketPlace CD-Rom (a customer database which Lotus were intending to sell on the open market), studied by Laura Gurak, these problems became quite apparent. In both cases it was industry groups who monopolized much of the online discussion to articulate and mobilize 'informed' opinion. But the communication practices 'promoted by the highly specialised nature of on-line communities [did] not always cultivate an open atmosphere', excluding those who did 'not assume or feel comfort-able with the prevailing community *ethos*' (Gurak 1999: 259–60). In both cases, those messages which were regarded as confirming the communities' suspicions were circulated extensively, while other less extreme messages or doubts as to the danger each technology really represented were merely ignored, and not forwarded around the group.

Being able to set the terms of the debate, to rule some things plau-sible and others as implausible (or 'uninformed'), has always been a major part of political power (Lukes 1974). The ability of some to impose their views, even in these new (virtual) communities, may indicate the continuing importance of prestige (although prestige itself may have changed in the realm of ICT-mediated networks).

Information might be an important resource, but there are many others, such as time, money and status. Moreover, power and influence are historically and institutionally anchored in law, policy, social and economic structures. . . . [I]nstitutions of governance have evolved through decades of negotiation and bargaining among con-flicting groups and interests to balance a variety of relationships within and between government and citizens. These social institutions are unlikely to be susceptible to radical change. (Dutton 1999: 59, 175)

The use of a new manner of communicating will hardly short-circuit these previous modes of power and influence. New ICTs may enhance certain aspects of political debate, they may allow new interests to be articulated, but this is in addition to the political structures we have already developed over centuries, and does not indicate their obsolescence.

Wider use of ICTs has not brought with it widespread political engagement. Research by the Pew Foundation suggests most of the interaction outside the workplace is between members of families or close personal groups of friends (reported in Naughton 2001). The resources of the internet are less often used for political activity, although as I noted above this is not necessarily unexpected. This falls short of the interactivity dreamt of in the visions of information politics. But hopes for this sort of interaction are hardly unprecedented: both the telegraph and the radio were predicted to transform the realm of interactive politics, but in the end they did not, or at least not in the ways that were predicted. Although they provided new ways of communicating, the opening up of political processes to wider deliberation which might have followed was successfully resisted by governments and their civil services. This is not to argue that the potential for political change is missing, but rather that it takes much more than a new technology to transform political practices.

Images, Gifts and Information Politics

Although I have so far focused on the internet, the political impact of the information society is part of a longer trend linked to the development of mass communications technologies. Manuel Castells perceives a 'crisis of democracy' connected to this trend, the result of the changing arena in which politics is played out:

> electronic media (including not only television and radio, but all forms of communication, such as newspapers and the Internet) have become the privileged space of politics. Not that all politics can be reduced to images, sounds or symbolic manipulation. But, without it, there is no chance of exercising or winning power . . . Outside the media sphere there is only political marginality. (1997a: 311–12)

While politics itself is *not* determined by the communications media, its characteristics influence the presentation and conceptualization of political information. Thus political leaders and groups wishing to be effective (or gain power) need to have an established media presence. For instance, much of Greenpeace's success has been the result of providing media-friendly stories and (most importantly) exciting images.

The relationship between the media, information and politics has changed the way politicians and political groups operate. Political parties have used feedback processes (such as focus groups) to inform and 'improve' their policies' presentation. Again, Castells points out that to 'understand the framing of politics by the logic of the media, we must refer to *the overarching principles governing news media: the race for audience ratings, in competition with entertainment; the necessary detachment from politics, to induce credibility'* (1997a: 321, emphasis in original). Conflicts, drama, disputes, betrayals and the revelation of secrets are required when the media's 'news values' are utilized to ensure that the bulletins and factual programmes broadcast are interesting and exciting. And 'because politics is personalized in a world of image making and soap operas, character assassination becomes the most potent weapon. Political projects, government proposals, and political careers can be undermined or even destroyed with the revelation of improper behaviour' (Castells 1997a: 323). This leads Castells to argue that information politics is the politics of scandal. Because of the focus on individuals (part of the individualization at the centre of the information society), the conduct of political actors has become more important and less private.

In scandal politics the media are constantly trying to find something newsworthy, and the slightest difficulty in presenting any action as legitimate may lead to a scandal, tying up political time in refutation and excuse. Where policy and personal behaviour are divergent, politicians are increasingly targeted. At the same time, as endless reports on the implications of policies and social trends garner press and media attention (provided they offer *newsworthy* conclusions), information about the private lives of politicians has become the subject of investigation, speculation and revelation. This move to personal morality and perceived hypocrisy has shifted debate in the media some way from the content of political actions and policy. As the internet has become more widely used, there has been a move to treat it like broadcast media. Political actors need to control the information they distribute and thus are unlikely to sponsor open forums (even if they monitor and evaluate popular opinion through electronic networks) (Castells 1997a: 351). Information is proffered as a resource to be used, not engaged with or modified through deliberative interaction. Despite this downbeat conclusion, in other areas of the information society there are some interesting 'political' things happening.

Linux, the gift economy and e-mutualism

One of the most discussed developments in the information society has been the open source software movement and its best-known example, the Linux operating system. Linux was originally a private research project by a Finnish computer studies student, Linus Torvalds. In 1991 he started to develop an operating system for his computer. Torvalds posted the kernel of his program, its central idea and software structure, on the internet and invited prospective users to improve it and (most importantly) share their improvements (Kollock 1999: 230). By 1994 it was sufficiently developed for Torvalds to take the decision to make it more widely available as version 1.0. and Linux was released under the general public licence pioneered by the Free Software Foundation: 'Its code, in other words, sits in the commons. Anyone can take it and use it as he wishes. Anyone can take it and understand how it works. The code of Linux is like a research programme whose results are always published for others to see. Everything is public; anyone, without having to seek the permission of anyone else may join the project' (Lessig 1999: 105). Though Torvalds still acts as the final coordinator for the project, its character of continual improvement allows each contribution to be monitored by others involved in the programme.

For many, this project and other open source developments are symbolic of the real politics of the information age, clearly demonstrating that the internet belongs to democratic technics. Linux emerged through the actions of one person initially but was swiftly enlarged and improved through the cooperative work of many others. This has been characterized as a 'gift economy'. In such an economy, the primary manner of obtaining things is through barter and gift. The bringing of a gift (in this case an improvement of Linux) allows you to enter a relationship with others where their (informational) gifts are available to you. The reciprocity of community has a real result: you contribute but receive much more in return. Linux is not part of a property regime, no one owns it and therefore people are motivated by their enjoyment of the problem solving rather than any financial benefit they might gain or forego by being part of the project (Kollock 1999: 231). This new space of gift giving, sharing and non-market exchange or use of (software) tools is therefore identified as an emergent political space outside capitalism.

Richard Barbrook has argued at length that this represents the internet-mediated beginnings of cyber-communism (Barbrook 2000). The political relations of sharing and gaining resources, alongside the widening use of ICTs, will enable this new space to expand and become a major political challenge to capitalist society. Eric Raymond, in a widely cited discussion, suggested that the difference between the old and the new was the difference between the 'cathedral and the bazaar'. In the old world, technological and other advances were developed by the few and disseminated to the many, in much the same way that religious teachings are communicated. However, Raymond's involvement in the development of Linux suggested to him that a new way of interacting was emerging: 'a great babbling bazaar of differing agendas and approaches ... out of which a coherent and stable system could seemingly emerge only by a succession of miracles' (Raymond 1998: 1). However, emerge it did, and it is this that has transformed the expectations from this new (political) domain, the information bazaar.

In this bazaar, information and knowledge are not traded but given away. Reputations are made and status accorded to those whose gifts are the most useful or elegant in their solution to a particular problem. In essence Raymond suggests that the internet has enabled the 'effective construction of voluntary communities of interest', which can and have produced excellent open-source software for the community (1998: 15). Here the community building eagerly searched for in the political sphere can be found. However, both Barbrook and Raymond recognize that this world operates in parallel to the world of 'normal' capitalist/market relations. They suggest that people will move between the two, making reputations in the gift economy which can then be translated into monetary rewards in the money economy. Only by working to support themselves in the property economy can the cyber-communists survive to maintain a presence in the gift economy. Given this dependence on the normal market relations it is linked to, this kind of gift economy, while certainly an additional political sphere, cannot at present be regarded as a major challenge to contemporary politics. But, the open source software movement may currently represent the most developed political alternative to 'normal' society, promoting a real e-mutualism (Thompson 2000: 32–3). It is a politics of doing, of actions, rather than debate and deliberation.

Bill Thompson suggests that we could choose e-mutualism in wider contexts than just in the production of software. Looking to the early history of the internet he argues that mutualism, rather than individualism, is (and has been) the way forward in the information society. The technology is 'naturally' supportive of mutualism, and if mutualism worked for those who developed the precursors to the internet, then it can be mobilized elsewhere. 'The barriers to successful co-operation are being torn down as a necessary part of the building of the digital village: in the world we are creating the potential for mutual endeavours is enhanced' (Thompson 2000: 42). Similarly, Charles Leadbeater suggests that the information society will usher in a new period when many social support mechanisms will be organized electronically and transferred to mutual societies 'owned' by their members. Communities will take over the organization of many of the welfare practices currently the responsibility of the state (Leadbeater 1999: 200). Rather than being constructed on the basis of 'tax and spend', the networks of the information society will be built on trust relationships, and they will arise from the group's communal relations rather than be imposed by authority.

In this new political space of individual interactions leading to some sort of modified, information mutualism we are left with the possibility that the real community that is emerging as characteristic of the information society is a community of individuals. While every community is made up of individuals, this new information community is individualized in the sense that the reasons for electing to join are the promotion of self-interest. This can be obscured by all sorts of claims regarding the greater good, but Raymond at least is explicit in his argument that the involvement in this sort of movement is a 'rational' response to the challenge of software development. While a collective response to complex problems is eminently sensible and rewards the individual disproportionately to their input, like nineteenth-century mutualism this new mutualism is a reaction to the problems of social fragmentation. This emphasizes the point that at the heart of the information age is a return of the sort of capitalism discussed by Marx and (temporarily) superseded by social and political developments in the second half of the twentieth century. And therefore, while hardly a compelling argument for the novelty of the information society, it does alert us to its most obvious political effect: the individualization of social existence.

Individualism in the Information Society

On one level, the new ICTs are being used to maintain social relationships established in 'real' space. But at the same time there is a growing awareness that the continuing deployment of ICTs seems to cause a decline in sociability. In 1998 researchers at Carnegie Mellon University reported that users of ICTs became socially isolated and their normal social interactions declined (Kraut et al. 1998). Subsequently there has been considerable disagreement over such conclusions and the effects on individuals who use new ICTs. It is probably too early to judge the psychological effects of prolonged reliance on internet interactivity to maintain social links (though this has not stopped many studies of varying quality and methodology from trying). Yet the thrust of the information society seems to be towards more individualized self-reliance. Certainly the individualized social actor is at the centre of much comment on the information society. In some respects this reflects more general political trends at the turn of the millennium, a down-playing of collectivities (especially class) and the conjectural emergence of individuals with particular interests as key sociopolitical actors. The move to locate responsibility for unemployment with the individual rather than with more general socioeconomic structural changes is exemplary of this trend.

This shift to individualism is in tension with civil society, the public realm which reflects more generalized social interests, whether these are articulated by interest groups, political parties, other organizations or individuals themselves. Indeed, while discussions of the information age often stress the individual acting on their own behalf, using new technologies to maximize their social benefits, this ignores or obscures the role shared norms might play in maintaining civility. Although analyses of the information society stress the coordination of social activity through market (and market-like) mechanisms, such methods of organization actually depend on extensive shared understandings, rules and social institutions (Hodgson 1999: 69ff.). While for many the sidelining of these institutions might free the individual from the constrictions of tradition, when individuals are 'freed' from these rules then civil society as a place of social interaction is also diminished. Respect for the values, interests and needs of others becomes of less importance, sacrificed on the altar of individualized attainment. This tension is clearly evident in the politics of intellectual property (see the appendix for an outline of what intellectual property is). Far from the deliberations and discussions of the academy, disputes about the character of the information society have come to life in the development and use of the MP3 music copying standard, and the software developed to take full advantage of its possibilities, such as Napster, and more recently Gnutella and Freenet.

Is copying CDs a political act?

The music industry very obviously relies on the knowledge content of the product to produce their profits, and so it is often seen as the prototypical information industrial sector. The reproduction of record companies' intellectual property at home by individuals has been a problem which has been exacerbated by successive new technologies (now including recordable CDs). Indeed, Simon Avenell and Herb Thompson have suggested that companies which develop and manufacture technologies enabling such actions are 'parasitic capitalists', surviving in direct tension with intellectual property producers (Avenell and Thompson 1994). The manufacturers of recordable CD technologies, and before them the developers of audio-cassette recording systems, can only profit through their customers' wanton disregard of the intellectual property encapsulated in another sector's products. The 'parasitic' product violates the commodity relationship (governed by intellectual property laws) established by the provider of entertainment goods or services. Ironically, with the consolidation of the entertainment and technology sectors, companies like Sony now find themselves on both sides. As owners of SONY/CBS, they deplore copying and piracy, but as manufacturers of Minidiscs, CD rewriters and cassette decks, they profit from it.

The re-recording of tracks on to cassette (or now CD) compilations or the recording of whole CDs for friends does not appear to the general public as an illegal activity. Plagiarism is generally frowned upon, and they are unlikely to pass off recordings as their own, but copying is seldom regarded as immoral. As with other material property, purchasers of CDs (and before that of vinyl records) usually believe that they are theirs to do with as they wish once they have paid the price asked – a view not shared by the copyright holders. Although few would necessarily extend their 'rights' to reproduction for sale, if they think about it at all most buyers of music products have no conception that aspects of home taping are regarded as unlawful (Litman 1991). Fair use doctrines, despite the best efforts of the music industry, have led courts to hold that individual re-recording does not contravene copyright, provided it is for one's own use (which is usually implicitly extended to giving it to a friend). Up until quite recently, and despite the fuss, the music industry has accepted home taping as a leakage of copyright it would tacitly ignore. However, the MP3 file format changed all that.

The MP3 file format was originally developed to allow sound to be compressed for easy downloading from websites. This was intended for original work to be distributed legally. Some companies set up websites where unsigned music acts could distribute their work to build a fan-base. But it was not long before users realized that they could copy their own CDs, upload them on to their computer and send music files to a friend, and soon an underground network of newsgroups (for technologically adept users) started to expand where files of commercial recordings could be found. Then Shawn Fanning thought it would be a good idea to produce a searchable database where his CD files could be stored and downloaded easily. In January 1999 he made the software he had developed (in his own time) at Boston's North West University available on the internet to anyone who might want to use it (Walsh 2000). The effect was that anyone could copy the CD-derived MP3 files he had loaded, as well as loading their own on to their own database. Suddenly, file swapping, which had up until then been a relatively specialized activity, became easy for anyone with access to a computer. Subsequently MP3 overtook sex as the most popular word used in search engines as file swapping accelerated (Curtis 2000). With broadband access (which allows greater capacity transfers in less time) the potential for 'sharing' software and films also expanded.

This led to two major developments. Napster itself became the subject of a large-scale legal dispute, and other software developers, seeing the way things were going, developed improved networking tools (Gnutella and Freenet) that required no central server to facilitate file swapping and thus made a legal challenge much harder. The case between Napster and Metallica (the band itself, and representing a number of other recording artists) heralded the decline of the company, but signalled to the industry that MP3 file swapping was not going to go away. All the major recording companies are in negotiations or have concluded deals which will enable them to take advantage of this technology. Currently the favoured business model seems to be unlimited downloads of the files maintained by a company, in exchange for a monthly subscription. The move to peer-to-peer computing, represented by Gnutella and Freenet, and initially a technical response to copyright policing, is now nominated as the future of computing, dispensing with the need for central server nodes and relying instead on extremely sophisticated network navigation software (Moores 2000). Things are moving quickly in this area and I do not want to go further into details that will surely be out of date by the time this book appears.

Nevertheless, we might suppose that these developments reveal the move to the gift economy heralded by Richard Barbrook and others. The notion that informational goods can be property is rejected, and in the rejection of property rights a clear political act is being committed. But, on the other hand:

> Of about 31,000 people who connected to the [Gnutella] system during the survey period [of twenty-four hours], 70% offered no files to download [in return for those they downloaded themselves]. And those who did share their collections [of CDs] did not contribute evenly. A mere 20% provided 98% of the material. Indeed the most generous 1% served up about 40% of it. (Economist 2000d)

Perhaps the gift economy is a little less public-spirited than its promoters suppose? A lot more receiving/taking than giving is evident. And if this is generally the case it is more difficult to argue that this is an explicit political act; rather it reflects a culture of individual wants being fulfilled without much concern for the effects. If the record industry and four hundred years of justifying copyright are right, without the possibility for reward, musicians will no longer want to produce music (see appendix). While many argue that there must be a way to ensure that some sort of reward is forwarded to successful artists (like shareware, we might all be asked to act in good faith and forward our royalties direct to the musicians), so far bands like Metallica seem unimpressed. On the other hand, in the history of human music-making, the period where it could be reproduced and sold for a profit has been rather short, effectively around seventy-five years; perhaps the information age will see a reversion to the making of music as a localized activity, with rewards centred on performance.

This relatively widely reported (and increasingly widespread) civil disobedience suggests that in the information society aspects of property rights have lost some of the legitimacy they may once have had. Since printing first emerged in the fifteenth century pirate editions and illegal copies have been a continuing problem for publishers (Johns 1998; Sell and May 2001), and therefore, in one sense, MP3 copying is merely the latest manifestation of this problem. However, the underlying logic of information as property is being challenged, not by an organized political campaign but by day-to-day acts which deny its legitimacy. We can imagine the political impact of large-scale trespass, or theft, on the material economy. Might this rebellion, at present lacking a political voice, yet have a major impact on the political structures of the information society?

While this is a pleasant thought for those seeking to find resistance to capitalism where they can, I am not so sure. On one level, copyright is clearly a central aspect of the information society's economy, and thus challenging it challenges the legitimacy of the structures of this society. But, with the exception of property in software (subject to a different sort of challenge from the open source movement), the property being 'stolen' is uniformly artistic, creative or cultural. Despite the outcry against prohibitively expensive patented AIDS drugs in Africa, there is still no concerted campaign to change the global trade agreement on intellectual property (the Trade Related Aspects of Intellectual Property Agreement (TRIPs) overseen by the WTO). The South African government's recent court victory over patents for AIDS drugs (and the legality of the generic alternatives it wanted to use) has been almost universally depicted as a necessary *exception* to the rule of intellectual property, rather than the beginning of the agreement's renegotiation or dissolution. And while non-governmental organizations and the environmental movement have been increasingly concerned about the patenting of genes and other bio-resources, popular civil disobedience has largely been limited to getting free music from the internet. Though intellectual property issues are symptomatic of the political problems with which the information society may be concerned, at least at present these thefts are only political acts by implication, not intent. This may change, and the possibilities of the internet have also allowed and encouraged more intentional politicized acts.

Individuals interacting

Accounts of information politics also frequently identify new arenas of expression and emerging avenues for the development of identity. Indeed identity politics and the manner in which we perceive ourselves as political beings are widely discussed as a major element in the emergence of the new communities of the information society. A not uncommon claim is that 'gender swapping [on the internet] is an extreme example of a fundamental fact: the network is in the process of changing not just how we work, but how we think of ourselves – and ultimately, who we are' (Bruckman 1996: 323). Much of the work which has celebrated the new fluidity of identity on the internet has revolved around the analysis of Multi-User-Dungeons/Domains (MUDs), a space for game-playing on the text-based internet which preceded the graphical revolution of the World Wide Web. The MUDs are frequently regarded as a new social space 'both like and radically unlike environments that have existed before' (Curtis 1996: 371). It is here that the potential to adopt a new identity is most developed, where users become indeterminate, remaking themselves (Dibbell 1999; Turkle 1997). Stories of gender-swapping, seduction and deception have become widespread and represent one of the most widely reported aspects of ICT-mediated social exchange in the mass media. But these communities may also allow the 'rediscovery' of identity, linking diaspora to 'home' countries, for instance. Emerging diasporic networks may find a political voice, and over issues such as human rights have already done so.

However, as Marek Kohn suggested above, in the realm of politics this (reported) fluidity makes it easier to ignore email interventions, or other ICT-mediated political communication, because of the ability to throw doubt on their authenticity. Campaigns based on email conducted by these new communities are often dismissed as the voices of (undemocratic) special interest groups rather than as those of the previously unheard. For instance, the recent anti-globalization campaigns have been branded as anti-democratic forces because their networked organization seems to indicate no formal representative function (Economist 2000e). The ability to mobilize without using a central organization has been turned against these 'movements' to indicate that they are unaccountable and should be ignored. By being a different sort of community,

some of the advantages of previous forms of political community
may be lost.

For Trevor Haywood, the difference between communities and
virtual communities is more than merely a different conduit for
the communications through which such groupings develop and
thrive:

> Society as it has operated in real space . . . has drawn out the great-
> est ideals and altruism from individuals who have diverted a part of
> their personal energy and resources to the common good, however
> capable they were of just looking after themselves. They did this
> because they inhabited and moved around the same spaces, shared
> the same problems and saw for themselves the variety of circum-
> stances and conditions that their neighbours experienced at first
> hand. We cannot, even with access to the most sophisticated virtual
> worlds, see or feel moved in the same way. (1998: 29)

The distancing which is integral to electronically mediated communication may well constrict the character of virtual communities.
Individualization is celebrated in much identity politics, ranging
from the ability to become someone 'new' to reacquaintance with
previously hidden aspects of the self. But this focuses politics on the
individual and away from a more collective notion of politics, away
from collective or community notions of responsibility.

However, where communication problems lead to prejudice, the
use of distanced ICT-mediated communication can be a real advantage (hence the abiding interest of feminists and anti-racists in
virtual communities). To take one example: for those with serious
hearing problems, the ability to communicate without revealing this
aspect of their life has opened up opportunities in work which were
previously closed, especially where such tasks can be fulfilled electronically. A Canadian study found that this has enabled some deaf
workers to side-step the discrimination they were exposed to, while
in the workplace the use of email has enhanced the social role
they can play in workplace politics (Lawson 2000). In a very real
way, the social space available to the deaf has been extended
and expanded. But although normal status indicators have been
removed, new forms of status have emerged, 'creating social hierarchies that can be every bit as restrictive and oppressive as some
in the corporeal world' (Reid 1998: 33). The notion that we can
choose any 'virtual identity' may be a little naive, as many factors

mediated by ICTs can influence and limit how we are perceived. This may range from speed of typing to the ability to express oneself succinctly or with ready wit. Any new identity may be less freely chosen than we think, as extended social interaction (even across the internet) tends to reveal much that we might try to conceal.

Surveillance, privacy and information politics

While the potential for a move to new networked identities is often proclaimed (and even may be quite real for many), the most obvious way ICTs have been developed to communicate and interact in the last few years has been e-commerce. This is not to argue that attempts to bring business to the internet have been overly successful. With some exceptions (of which Amazon, Yahoo and eBay are perhaps the most obvious), e-commerce has hardly been an unalloyed success. Nevertheless, rather than an explosion of female oriented sites proclaiming a new period of feminism, for instance, there has been a proliferation of 'lifestyle' sites. In America, where female internet users have surpassed men, the most visited sites are pampers.com, avon.com and oilofulay.com. Even sites like Women.com admit that most visits are for the sections on 'sex tips' and horoscopes, hardly political issues (Summerskill 2000). Although there is a lot of explicitly political content on the internet, from individual homepages to campaigning sites, these are by no means the most frequently viewed. Even where new communities *have* arisen, their collective articulation is often through an aspect of consumption, buying a service, discussing how to modify products (as in software discussion groups) or relating to a pastime that frequently involves products, services or events provided through the market. The use of information collected in these 'communities' has led to concerns about privacy.

The collection of information about customers has long been a by-product of commercial transactions. From crude measures of what is selling, to sophisticated manipulation of customer details, companies have always tried to 'know' their customer. Loyalty schemes in shops lead to customer databases of information about our private practices and tastes, while credit card companies hold similar records for an increasing proportion of our transactions (as we use our cards more often). The proliferation of information about habits and consumption may have a political effect as the proliferation of scandals suggests, but these effects are also evident in the lives of those outside the realm of public affairs. Our ability to remain anonymous, to retain our privacy, is being eroded by the information society. Indeed, sometimes it seems as though consumer information has developed a life of its own, with a large market for such information emerging. Where diverse data can be coordinated (public records and purchased databases), considerable and revealing information sets can be constructed, unknown to the subjects of these originally separate records. This represents the most obvious aspect of the increased possibilities for surveillance that have been developed in recent years, part of what Kevin Robins and Frank Webster have called 'the dark side of the information revolution' (1999: 94ff.). The deployment of powerful ICTs has heightened the possibility of monitoring and control by the state (and other powerful groups) which contrasts with the empowerment of the individual often presented as typical of the information age.

A common assumption among those who are less worried about privacy in the information society is that as we all get used to more and more information about us being publicly available, and as this is the same for everyone, we will become less concerned about it (Dyson 1997: 216–17; Raab et al. 1996: 293). Implicitly we may accept a trade-off between the ability of commercial organizations to treat us as individuals (by knowing about us from our previous transactions), and the erosion of privacy this may entail. This may be why, despite the clear privacy issues, in Britain the Labour government's recent Regulation of Investigatory Powers Bill failed to engender a popular campaign of protest. The liberties being eroded by the bill's provisions (maintaining secret encryption keys, confidentiality of emails) have yet to raise any popular interest (Naughton 2000c). On the one hand too few people may be affected, but on the other even those who are already using these technologies may not understand their workings well enough to realize what is possible. Increasingly ICTs are being used to monitor the very information flows they have encouraged and facilitated.

I have already noted the possibilities of oversight in the informationalized workplace, but it is not only at work that problems are evident. New modes of surveillance are made possible by deploying the latest ICTs, but surveillance itself is not a direct result of these technologies. Rather, it is the increased recognition of risk and better information about the world in which we live, alongside the continuing relations of political power, which have supported widened surveillance (Lyon 2001). The development of scientific knowledge has revealed causal links between behaviour and unwelcome occurrences (such as the link between smoking and cancer or the effects of certain diets) and this has shifted much of life from the realm of luck to the realm of the social control of risk. We can monitor our diets, we recognize the dangers of pollution and we can take action. Thus better information equips us (and society) better to recognize risk.

The monitoring of everyday lives (by ourselves or others) may seem more legitimate than in the past (think of the questions you are happy to answer when applying for credit or insurance), not least of all as information requests have become relatively normalized through continued repetition by different organizations and agencies. However, because there is so much 'disorganized' surveillance, the surveillance that can be used for control or discipline is partly obscured by the general growth of information holding by organizations (Lyon 2001: 35–6). From companies to governments, more and more information is gathered and can be used in ways which might not have been clear when the original details were submitted. Therefore, Manual Castells suggests, we need be less wary of 'big brother' and should instead turn to the activities of what he terms the 'little sisters' (1997a: 299–303). While governments remain (at least potentially) accountable to their citizens, this is less the case for the private sector. Not all uses of the information gathered will necessarily be objectionable, but equally it is difficult to claim that *none* will be.

The ability of ICTs to generate comprehensive records of use, and the ways these records are used, has therefore become a central concern for civil-libertarians. But perhaps the greatest concern is about the general ignorance among users of the violation of their privacy. Paul Schwartz points out:

> Visitors to cyberspace sometimes believe they will be fully able to choose among anonymity, semi-anonymity and complete disclosure of identity and preferences. Yet in each of the three areas, finely granulated personal data are created – often in unexpected ways. Moreover, most people are unable to control, and are often in ignorance of, the complex processes by which their personal data are created, combined and sold. (1999: 1621–2)

In one sense the storing of customer contact information is relatively unproblematic; those from whom we buy services and products always know something about us due to these interactions. But, records held by internet service providers and other websites can also provide complex clues about one's activities through records of internet usage. Coordinating this with information regarding off-line activities (but available online, from electoral roles for instance) can further enhance personal profiles without the knowledge or permission of their subjects. This surveillance is becoming more widespread (if still relatively unrecognized) and thus joins work-place monitoring as part of a wider concern for individual privacy in the information age.

Despite the usual mantra that 'the innocent have nothing to hide', given the strongly individualist ideology of the internet the inva-sion of privacy by (potential) monitoring has become a high-profile issue among specialist discussion groups, although this has yet to make a mark on more traditional politics. One response is for users to learn how to navigate around the 'virtual world' without leaving a trace, and already some people are taking advantage of anonymiz-ing software to do this. It has also led those suspicious of ever more 'informed' government to establish communities that seek to reduce or obliterate the records of their existence by dealing in cash, by not registering to vote, by becoming part of the shadow economy, or as American survivalists put it, 'going off the grid'. More invidiously, although monitoring of many sorts may help catch criminals, it may also catch much circumstantial behaviour that can be read either as innocent or criminal. The logic of monitoring requires the innocent to disabuse the watcher of their suspicions, to prove that there is an innocent explanation for the monitored activity (Lessig 1999: 152). If we do not wish to offer an explanation for our ability to conduct a perfectly legal transaction, say buying a house for cash, once we have fallen under suspicion through the collation of circumstantial evidence our innocence is no longer presumed. Rather we have to offer a counter-explanation to the authorities to ward off further investigation, or even prosecution on the balance of probability of guilt.

While, in the past, collating the information to build a profile or even gaining access to information was relatively difficult, requir-ing skills and deception beyond the abilities (or will) of many, cheap and powerful computing has lowered the barriers to access, a view popularized in the media with stories of personal records being wiped to make individuals 'non-persons'. Indeed, in popular cul-ture the threats of information retrieval by criminals and others aiming to cause harm have become commonplace in films like *Enemy of the State*. In the real world, once we all know a little more about the technological issues, the right to privacy may become *the* politics of the information age. As an issue it dovetails with the increasingly individualized lives we are told are part of the information society, and therefore the invasive character of information holdings may become less acceptable to *private* individuals. Certainly, where the control of information by government is concerned, the libertarian (Californian) ideology of much of the writing on the internet regards this as a serious danger. But, on the other hand, where the state holds information on residences of convicted paedophiles, and there is a perceived risk to children, for instance, suddenly rights to privacy seem to be less important to the public.

Equally, there has been little outcry and considerable support for closed circuit TV (CCTV) monitoring of city centres as a crime reduction strategy. The usual justification of this surveillance has been based on reducing the risk of crime. While there is always the danger of displacement (criminals may merely move to other areas), there is also the lingering notion that like children at school we are being 'watched over' to ensure we behave because some of us cannot be trusted. And where the line between good behaviour and criminality is argued over (recently for instance in anti-capitalist demonstrations), the use of CCTV to monitor crowds, identify 'trouble-makers' and to provide images as evidence for subsequent prosecutions emphasizes the ability of surveillance to discipline certain sections of society.

> Surveillance power is often wielded in ways that systematically disadvantage some groups rather than others, but this can be a side-effect of policies meant to achieve other ends. The biggest obstacle in the path of resistance [to the surveillance society] is the rather mundane fact that the benefits of surveillance are attractive to many, and well promoted. (Lyon 2001: 136)

Thus movement records may be a by-product of mobile telephone network maintenance. In 1997 it was revealed that Swisscom, the Swiss network, kept records of movements of mobile phone handsets (data generated by the system to allow call connection to be initiated). This information was not only stored but made available to the police (Steffik 1999: 215). Although ultimately declared illegal by the Swiss Privacy Commission and the country's parliament, the existence of such records implies a large store of information about personal movements which many of us might regard as invasive.

Balancing the civil liberties of different groups has never been easy and this is just as evident in the 'new' information society, not least of all as there is a broadening of the available information over which conflicts may occur. Michael Dertouzos, long-time head of MIT's Laboratory for Computer Science, suggests that this reveals the continued need for government. The choice for the citizens of the information society is 'whether they want to be the ones controlling the privacy of their communications or whether they are willing to share this right with their governments in order to protect themselves from criminal and enemy activities' (Dertouzos 1997: 225). If the politics of the information society continues to focus on risk avoidance and the danger of criminality, information politics as a resistance to the 'surveillance society' is likely to remain underdeveloped. Although there have been considerable legal efforts to ensure that surveillance is in some way accountable, the balance still seems to lie with the second of Dertouzos's possibilities. Of course, the fear of (cyber)criminal activity itself may be whipped up by politicians and others who wish to continue or expand opportunities for surveillance. Law and order, a far from new issue in politics, will have as great a role to play in information politics as it has in the past. The threats which politicians (and sometimes the police) constantly emphasize may be different, but the 'need' for oversight to enhance security remains.

Communicating Politics

Given that the main aspect of information age politics concerns the communication of information, the internet may be only 'an extension of the fax machine, the telephone, the postal system, the picket fence and cable television in being a medium of political communication . . . a supplement to political discourse, not a gigantic paradigm shift' (Hill and Hughes 1998: 179). Indeed, it is merely an extension of the book, the pamphlet, the daily newspaper as an arena for political discussion. Hill and Hughes conclude that rather than the emergence of a new politics, 'people will mould the internet to fit traditional politics' (1998: 186). Certainly, with the possible exception of surveillance and issues of individual privacy, there has yet to emerge a campaign that is politically unprecedented, although some of the agitation around encryption technologies might become an important information age political dispute. The use of ICTs by already established political campaigns and groups has enhanced their efficacy in certain ways, but it has not transformed their practices. They still try to mobilize large groups and use public opinion as a counterweight to government administrations, although this may now be undertaken via email. Like previous technologies from the telegraph and telephone to the radio and television, politics is more likely to adapt to these new forms of communication than undergo a major shift.

The arrival of information politics is perhaps better dated to the move to mass literacy, universal suffrage and the rise of the mass media over one hundred years ago. The plurality that is often claimed for the new information politics already existed at the end of the nineteenth century. As Andrew Chadwick has argued, the 'popular' element of politics was enhanced by 'a public sphere of print communications . . . in which the "mainstream" press was accompanied by a diverse range of marginal and oppositional newspapers, journals and pamphlets, all supported by a variety of literate publics' (1999: 45). It was during this period that the widespread move from oral to text-based communication took place and this would seem a more profound remaking of the political than the widening ability to communicate texts (and the ease of producing them for distribution) characteristic of the contemporary information age. Although its arrival is frequently compared with the printing revolution, at present I see little in the information age to compare with the profound expansion of available information in the fifty years after Gutenberg printed the first Bible using movable type. Rather, new ICTs have enhanced, expanded or accelerated the forms of communication already available. The quantitative acceleration produced by the deployment of ICTs is confused with the profound (qualitative) changes in social and political practices which can be traced to the advent of printing (see Eisenstein 1980).

There may have been some change in the forms of communication of politics, and there has certainly been some enhancement of the ability to organize quickly (how permanent an advantage this is remains to be seen), but as far as the subject-matter of politics goes and the sorts of groups who conduct its central interactions, there is little to suggest an important disjuncture. Indeed, there are, as there have always been, gatekeepers to information sources – discussion group moderators, webmasters and others – who may subtly (or sometimes not so subtly) amend or limit the information available, or the communications posted. Even in the most 'democratic' groups there are modes of interactions which if breached can lead to expulsion or messages being deleted. Furthermore, with continuing functional literacy problems in many countries, any text-based medium will have a limited reach, even if many pages have some image content. Neither have previous media been outmoded or side-stepped by these new modes of information dissemination. Indeed, older media (especially newspapers) have used the appearance of stories on the internet to justify publication, on the basis that they are only repeating what has already appeared in the public realm. In cases regarding British 'state secrets' this has become a reasonably robust defence (as the Tomlinson and Shayler cases have shown). In the realm of politics, ICT-mediated interaction seems (at least so far) to have been an additional aspect to communities' networks rather than a replacement for them.

Although there is a potential to enhance democratic deliberation, not everyone wants to expand their involvement in politics. The internet, as the realm in which information politics has been expected to emerge, and despite hopes for an expansion in participation, has done little to transform the character of politics, because people's interests remain outside the formal political realm. It has enabled some groups to enhance their campaigning and organization, but it has not led to a new politics. While there are possibilities for new identity formation and the emergence of new communities, these remain firmly connected with the real world of our lives either through the replication of social structures and behaviour or because their concerns are with the world in which we live. To echo Calhoun, we need to look at society first and ask what role ICTs are playing in politics, not presume that the politics we find on the internet *is* information age politics. While it has enhanced the communicative possibilities open to everyone (everyone 'connected', that is), at present at least the information age has not led to a profound transformation of political activity.

5

W(h)ither the State?

I now turn to the last area where I am sceptical regarding claims for the emergence of the (global) information society. The suggestion that states and their governments are likely to decline in importance in the information age is mistaken. Quite the contrary: not only is the role of the state less compromised by information and communication technologies (ICTs) than is often presumed, but states also play a major and important role in facilitating the types of activities that some believe render them obsolete. While the practices of states and governments may be changing, this is not the same as a general decline in importance.

Currently there is significant planning related to the information society taking place in Europe despite the frequent assertion that such activities are both pointless and outmoded (Servaes and Burgelman 2000: 4). At the same time that the information society is supposed to be sidelining the state, its construction requires interventions by the state, although these may be different from previous state policies. And, Steve Fuller suggests, 'historically the only reliable way to prevent the introduction of a new technology from *redrawing* existing class divisions in society has been government regulation' (1998: 129, emphasis added). This is why the attempts to sideline issues of class I discussed in chapter 3 are linked to arguments for a reduced role for government in the information society. If class is presented as no longer important, then the role of the state can be regarded as less vital. Thus many writers foster a public discourse of information society (allied to globalization) which promotes as a truism the inevitable marginalization of the state and a decreasing utility of governmental intervention, alongside the displacement of the importance of any *particular* location. However, the state continues to play a key role in facilitating the deployment and use of ICTs in social relations, as well as itself using these technologies to support its own capabilities, and in this respect geography remains significant.

Early Views of the State in the Information Age

In the first wave of writing on the information society the role of the state was regarded as less problematic than in more recent declarations of its decline. Writing in the early 1970s, Daniel Bell predicted that in the information age, economic decisions would be subordinated to 'other forces in society; the crucial decisions regarding the growth of the economy and its balance will come from government but they will be based on the government's sponsorship of research and development, of cost-effectiveness and cost benefit analysis.' Despite calls for widened political participation, Bell argued that while democracy was valuable, it was crucial that guidance was provided by an elite of experts (1974: 344, 366). Technocrats, mobilizing their specialized knowledge through state institutions, would facilitate the emergence of an information and knowledge driven postindustrial society. This stemmed from the 'simple fact that knowledge and planning – military planning, economic planning, social planning – have become the basic requisites for all organised action in modern society' (Bell 1974: 362). The rule of an elite would support an equitable and virtuous society, and would avoid the erosion of liberty by populism and faction. Bell's information society was based on the rule of experts, whose knowledge was technical and thus depoliticized.

Bell's view that the state's role would be directive was well received in France, where dirigism (the extensive involvement of the state in the economy) has a long and distinguished history. But even here analysts suggested government should 'develop tools to make their policy work by acting with strength where power relationships dominate the scene, and by restricting their actions and decentralizing when needed changes require other groups to take the initiative' (Nora and Minc 1980: 9). Although the balance may be different from some contemporary opinion, Simon Nora and Alain Minc were already arguing for the limitation of state activities to those areas where the state could produce efficient solutions to problems, leaving the rest of the information society's development to non-governmental, commercial agents (Nora and Minc: 117–23). This idea of a permissive state, guiding with a 'light touch', persists as a central element in many treatments of information age, the area of contention being how light a touch will promote the desired ends.

In 1980 it seemed possible that the state could free markets from the domination of large companies as part of guiding them. Simon Nora and Alain Minc suggested to the French President that 'state activity cannot be limited to installing a public data transmission system and broadening access to it. It is necessary to free the users from the manufacturers' monopoly over the design of large systems architectures' (1980: 102). While free markets were a key aspect of the information society, they were unlikely to remain 'free' without the regulatory authority of the state to forestall monopoly. On the other hand, Nora and Minc's report, *The Computerization of Society*, also stressed the role of the government as a service provider itself, and the possibility that state utilization of ICTs could engender increased take-up in French society more generally. The report, among other things, led the French state to support Minitel, which, while locking many consumers into a non-internet technology in the mid-1990s, produced an acceptance of networking which underpinned a massive acceleration of French internet connectivity at the turn of the millennium. But the report also recognized the difficulty (or even impossibility) of the government organizing a particular trajectory for the information society. While facilitating the deployment of ICTs, governments were unlikely to be able to decide exactly in what direction developments would proceed.

Well before the internet began to reach out across the global system, the very idea of a network of computers led Wilson Dizard to warn that it 'took a half-century to sort out the economic, legal and social aspects of a relatively simple integrated phone system. These factors are immensely more complex in the new network, with its expanded capability for voice, visual and data services' (Dizard 1982: 38). On one hand, this implied a major role for the state to 'sort out' these issues. But on the other, Dizard suggested that the state should support the *commercial* development of the nascent network: 'Driven by economic forces, the new networks can expand beyond business and government services into the consumer sector' (1982: 40–1). This did not imply that the state's involvement would be insignificant; rather the government and private sector would work together to further the development of the information society. While private commercial organizations were to play a major role, this would be in conjunction *with*, not apart from (or even in tension with), a continuing role for the state.

Around the same time, Tom Stonier regarded the state as important not only as the regulator and supplier of social services but also as a key investor in emergent and capital intensive technologies (1983: 84–98). More recent writers seem to have forgotten the major role governments played in the development of the internet and biotechnology (the sectors most often taken as paradigmatic of the information age), but Stonier regarded these state investments as a key factor in supporting the emergence of the information society. On the other hand, not all early writers on the information society saw the continuity of government involvement in society as valuable or desirable. In his critical discussion of 'post-industrial utopians' (stretching from André Gorz to Alvin Toffler), Boris Frankel (1987) derides them for presuming that the postindustrial society would lead to the emergence of a 'stateless society'. In this early critical literature it was often hoped that moves towards the information society would lead to a withering away of the state as information flows allowed a more spontaneous, less power-dependent coordination of society. What draws these writers together is a suspicion of and antagonism towards the domination of politics by states and their governments: for them the state was the agent of the oppressing power of capital. However, this left-inspired criticism of the role of the state in the information age has subsequently been developed and extended by writers from the right.

From a right-of-centre perspective, the information age (and specifically the internet) represents a chance to sideline government and reconstitute a voluntary society of responsible individuals, whose interactions are facilitated by a 'neutral' market. Even writers with less extreme views of the problem of a 'strong state' have argued that it is being eclipsed by the sort of social relations prompted by the widening use of ICTs. From Esther Dyson and Don Tapscott in America to Diane Coyle and Charles Leadbeater in Britain, writers suggest that the state can no longer keep up with the social innovations of the information society. It is not only that states should stop trying to shape the future and withdraw from many areas of policy-making: even if governments want to, they are actually *unable* to continue to play the socioeconomic role they played in the second half of the twentieth century. So, while early commentary often saw a relatively important and continuing role for the state in some form, the subsequent thrust of discussion has regarded the role of the state as *necessarily* diminishing.

Sidelining the State

Twenty years ago, one of the key demands in the debates around the McBride Report's argument for a New World Information and Communication Order was for the 'right to communicate' (MacBride et al. 1980). To 'democratise communication' it was necessary to 'ensure that facilities are made available to individuals and various social groups for the interchange of information on a more equal footing' (Ansah 1986: 78). The internet has been seized upon as finally enabling the establishment of this democratic communicative medium. Whereas the ownership of the mass media has long been a problem for the free discussion of political issues in many parts of the international system, the internet (potentially) allows greater possibilities for communication among interested parties (as discussed in the last chapter). Politics has thrown off the shackles of the state and a new globalized civil society is emerging.

Additionally, despite the economically interventionist state being of relatively recent vintage (at its strongest in the second half of the twentieth century), there are also widespread proclamations that the information age already makes it obsolete. The globalization of the economy, alongside the technological character of the information society, constrains the ability of states' governments to maintain independent economic and fiscal policies. The power and authority previously enjoyed by the state has been transferred to (or captured by) the private, commercial sector. Furthermore, it is argued, as the important resources of capitalism have become more related to knowledge and information, so the reliance on specific locations as bases of economic activity for the utilization of these resources has declined. Therefore, although the period of globalization after the Second World War seemed still to allow some element of choice for governments in their responses to economic events, contemporary globalization underpinned by the information revolution has curtailed or even removed such choices (Thurow 2000: 30). The information age challenges the efficacy of the state in both the political and economic realms where it had previously enjoyed (albeit variable) sovereignty.

Economic challenges to state efficacy

It is frequently noted that as assets and products become increasingly informational, territorial space is less important; key resources for economic success are no longer relatively fixed in specific locations. Using new and powerful ICTs, corporations can easily organize themselves on the basis of international or even global networks rather than national production systems. National borders have been breached and no longer shape economic relations as they did in the past, famously leading Kenichi Ohmae to suggest that we now live in a new 'borderless world' (Ohmae 1990). Thus Jessica Mathews affirmed a widespread assumption when she argued that

> technology has been a driving force, shifting financial clout from states to the market with its offer of unprecedented speed in transactions . . . governments have only the appearance of free choice when they set economic rules. Markets are setting de facto rules enforced by their own power. States can flout them, but the penalties are severe – loss of vital foreign capital, foreign technology and domestic jobs. Even the most powerful economy must pay heed. (1997: 57)

Utilizing complex ICT-mediated networks, multinational companies (MNCs) are able to evade regulation and taxation by states' governments, while establishing a global market for their goods and services. Facing this shift, states are increasingly helpless, no longer able to 'protect' particular economic sectors or groups from the rigours of the global market.

Although the progressive dismantling of capital controls by states themselves facilitated this easy international mobility of financial capital, powerful ICTs linked to a global network have enhanced (or aggravated) this effect by making such transfers instantaneous and ever more difficult to detect, dissolving state authority. Indeed, the possibility of tracking capital flows for regulatory purposes has declined in direct relation to the ability to move funds at the touch of a button. Furthermore, this is costly to the state exchequer: for instance, the use of tax havens by MNCs to 'hide' profits may cost poor countries up to $50 billion a year (Denny 2000). It has therefore become a commonplace that the ability of states to raise funds or regulate economic activities through market intervention has been severely reduced. In the realm of fiscal policy, interstate competition has diminished the possibility of operating regulatory regimes that are considerably different from the 'accepted norm' and has led to a downward trend in 'acceptable' levels of taxation and regulation. Some variance in policy is possible but only within certain limited parameters if much-needed investment by MNCs is to be attracted. States need MNCs much more than companies need specific states, and the competition to attract such economic powerhouses has led to the adoption of policies governments suppose these companies favour (Strange 1996, 1998). Additionally, 'unwelcome' policy adjustments or revelations may lead to swings in currency markets, destabilizing exchange rates (as in the Asian financial crisis of the late 1990s). The globalized information age prompts a decline in state efficacy, robbing it of fiscal tools and funds.

Unable to direct the economy, governments have to work with other actors at local and global levels, causing state authority to be further diluted. Manuel Castells argues that states, 'having become part of a network of powers and counter powers, are powerless by themselves: they are dependent on a broader system of enacting authority and influence from multiple sources'(1997a: 305). Esther Dyson's 'design for living in the Digital Age' does not include a major role for the state because the 'digital world is a new terrain . . . [and] is almost impossible for traditional governments to regulate' (1997: 6). Even when a role is recognized, it may be minimal: Bill Gates suggests 'governments can help determine the "rules of the road", the guidelines within which companies compete, but they shouldn't try to design or dictate the nature of the network because governments aren't very good at outguessing the competitive marketplace' (1996: 280). The state should take a permissive rather than a directive role.

Thus states may no longer be the ideal agents for political activity in societies either. Peter Evans surmises: 'Legitimate disillusionment with the state's capacity to deliver, exacerbated by the pervasive anti-state discourse of the Anglo-American global order, has solidified into a domestic political climate that makes engaging the state as an ally seem farfetched' (1997: 86). Or as Lester Thurow succinctly suggests: 'If national governments cannot protect their citizens economically, why should their citizens support them politically?' (2000: 23). If the state is unable to deliver the sorts of economic benefits it did in the past, then it is not only its economic efficacy that is being challenged by the information society.

Political challenges to state efficacy

Drawing strength from the Jeffersonian roots of the Californian ideology, the libertarianism of many writers on the information society
prompts the identification of the state as a threat to liberty (Barbrook and Cameron 1996). For instance, Phiber Optik, a hero of
the hacking community in the early 1990s, who cracked computer
codes to access phone networks without charge, declared: 'People
tend to think that the government has a lot to fear from a rebellious
hacker lashing out and destroying something, but we think we
have a lot more to fear from the government because it is within
their power to take away everything we own and throw us in jail'
(quoted in Rushkoff 1994: 264). What some might see as the state's
legitimate activity of protecting the rights of telephone companies
to charge for the use of their assets, Optik portrays as the imposition of a powerful and unjust state machine, infringing his individual rights.

In America even the provision of welfare is regarded by some
as an imposition of state authority on the individual citizen. This
position has a long pedigree, not least of all in political arguments
against universal health provision and for the promotion of individual responsibility for welfare. Libertarianism may see a continuing role for the state, but *contra* Optik, this is largely limited to the
protection of property rights (Calabrese 1997: 15; Dyson et al. 1994).
Attacks on the welfare state, a staple of right-leaning politics for
many years, have gained strength by linking up with the less 'political', more 'technical' recognition of an emerging global information society. When joined to the Californian ideology, arguments
against the state prompt calls for the control or limitation of government 'interference' in the workings of society. In the world
outside America, however, the authority of the state is a much more
serious problem.

For commentators like Walter Wriston, echoing claims made by
Marshall McLuhan in the 1960s, the information society will engender a global village which will enjoy a global culture and customs:
'Denying people human rights or democratic freedoms no longer
means denying them an abstraction never experienced, but violating the established customs of the village ... [and thus] an enormous burden of proof falls on those who would deny [these rights]'
(Wriston 1997: 175). The communication of information about alternatives empowers those living in oppressive states to see that their

plight is not inevitable, while outward information flows can stimulate the mobilization of political forces to pressure governments through diplomacy and political organization. This has prompted a globalization of oppositional campaigns. The internet offers a space, previously unavailable, for dissent from authoritarian and totalitarian regimes (or perhaps more accurately a space where those outside the country can see dissent more clearly than in the past). The Chinese dissident community, for instance, runs a number of online newsgroups which disseminate information about political opposition in China and allow domestic dissidents to maintain contact with their ideological (and financial) supporters abroad. Domestic groups mobilize through email (relatively anonymously) as well as through newly available mobile phone networks. China's current 'problem' with the Falun Gong spiritual movement has been made more public and more intractable through the movement's widespread use of these networks. Their leader has been able not only to help coordinate and support actions, but also to publicize the struggle outside China quite effectively, despite being held by the US Immigration and Naturalization Service in Guam.

Elsewhere, in an attempt to quash discussion of civil service corruption, the Singapore government closed down 127 internet cafés for lacking licences and 'corrupting the minds of young people', although this was explicitly turned into an issue of pornography rather than the ability to access oppositional political content. However, this has done little to stem the flow of revelations discussed at home or abroad (Schmit and Wiseman 2000). Indeed, censorship has always been a supremely political act based on legitimized state authority, even when this has concerned publications identified as pornographic (Thomas 1969). The current heated debates around the dissemination of cyber-porn (and most specifically pornography involving children) have again revealed the difficulty for national regulators in stemming the flows of material regarded as repugnant. Internet service providers (ISPs) within a state's territory may be held responsible and fined or closed down, but the very character of the internet allows access to non-national ISPs.

Legal focus has therefore shifted to possession: cached images on a hard disc (for distribution or the holder's own use) have led to some successful prosecutions under national laws. But using possession as the locus of sanction hardly offers encouraging support for attempts to control these flows of information. The example of drug use (and criminal distribution), another area where possession is the easiest point to prosecute, suggests the potential problem for state-level policing. Despite considerable investment in policing and social legislation, drug use in all developed states continues to expand. Governments also continue to use legislative methods with regard to official secrets, but as the 'revelations' of David Shayler and Richard Tomlinson showed, cross-border breaches of secrecy are difficult to contain or halt, especially once the information has appeared on the internet. The issuing of a D-notice to proscribe publication in Britain merely alerted many elements of the press to the actual location of the secrets Tomlinson was alleged to have 'made public'. The ability of the state (or its representatives) to block unpalatable information flows has been greatly diminished by the fluid nature of internet connections, and once access has been allowed, trying to control that access is almost impossible for government agencies.

In struggles like those in East Timor, the ability to bypass 'official' media, to quickly publicize ongoing violations of human rights and to use ICTs to mobilize international response swiftly has certainly changed the environment in which oppressive governments operate (Metzl 1996). But it is not only the internet which has enabled these sorts of pressure to build up against authoritarian states. Mass communication networks and the broadcast of programmes such as the Voice of America and the BBC's World Service played a seemingly significant (if difficult to define) role in the oppositional politics of Eastern Europe and Russia during the 1970s and 1980s, leading to the 'velvet revolutions' which saw the public rise against oppressive states. From international telephone calls to radio transmissions, the alternative to these regimes became better known and this enhanced the possibility of mobilization for political change. Whether the internet will have a similar effect on regimes from Myanmar or Zambia to hardline Islamic governments remains to be seen. Interestingly the struggle over the reform movement in Iran has involved the widespread use of the media, and while the conservative elements in the state have mobilized the apparatus of law and order to contain the discussion of intended reforms, protesters continue to resurface. Ayatollah Khomeni's pre-Revolutionary campaigning was largely conducted through the distribution of audio-cassettes of his sermons, and now the reform movement in contemporary Iran is using the internet to side-step some of the repression targeted at opposition papers and other media.

The 'death of distance' and 'the end of geography'

All this goes some way to support Wriston's assertion that the information revolution is starting to profoundly threaten 'the power structures of the world' (1997: 175). This stretches from the problems of control being experienced by authoritarian states to the political challenges which have limited governmental intervention in the rich and developed countries. In the information society the state is presented as of increasingly marginal importance to both political and economic relations. At its most developed, this argument asserts that while previously the geography of the world was important, in the information age the impact of distance on communication (and therefore on other socioeconomic relations) has been radically reduced by the widespread utilization of ICTs. Using the terminology of geography, it is often asserted that a 'new space' has developed in addition to the more usually recognized space in which nation-states are arrayed in the international system: this new space is 'cyberspace'. Whereas in the past space seemed to have a predominantly physical character (organized into countries), cyberspace exists within the electronic networks and commercial organizations that have spread across the world, and is no longer linked to specific locations.

Ten years ago these developments led Richard O'Brien of American Express to proclaim the 'end of geography' (O'Brien 1992). More recently Frances Cairncross of the *Economist* has declared the 'death of distance': 'Historically, the size of political units has mostly been determined by geography . . . The death of distance will not only erode national borders; it will reduce the handicaps that isolation has previously imposed on countries on the fringes of economic regions' (1998: 258). The location of economic activity will become less crucial, allowing those outside the developed world to enter markets which previously might have been difficult to access because of practical problems of communication and lack of interaction. Indeed, Diane Coyle has suggested that 'a growing share of economic activity does not have any national physical location at all' (1997: 18), while Michael Dertouzos claims distance is no longer 'measured in kilometres but in keystrokes and other electronic gestures' (1997: 277). Such pronouncements have become a cliché of globalization and also figure widely in discussions of the impact of ICTs on the world in which we live.

In our social relations, this position asserts that we 'are released from the limitation of geographic proximity as the sole basis of friendship, collaboration, play and neighbourhood . . . drawing people into a greater world harmony' (Negroponte 1995: 230). And as Cairncross emphasizes, 'individuals everywhere will know more about the ideas and aspirations of human beings in every other part of the world, thus strengthening the ties that bind us all together' (1998: 26, 277–99). This long-standing liberal idea, that better communication between the global population will lead us to recognize our global commonality, suggests that politically particular locations (or 'place') will become less crucial as we all become global citizens. Thus, in the information age, as obstructions to communication fall, so the realization of a globalized humanity living in a single location (earth) becomes possible. The nation-state as a container for our hopes and needs will be eclipsed as increasingly we look to non-national networks for our social identity and well-being. While Cairncross herself admits that this may be an optimistic scenario, she suggests that the divisions which have stemmed from the organization of the world into national spaces (ruled by national authorities) will be a thing of the past (1998: x). The world will become, in a phrase coined by Marshall McLuhan in the 1960s, a 'global village'.

However, this is not to suggest that all locations are therefore equal. This decline of specific locational advantage opens up the possibility of economic competition between locations (and their governors, both regional and national) to attract inward investment, often at the cost of tax revenues. Thus states, no longer able to offer unique resources, will need to compete in global markets on the basis of the costs of economic activity within their borders. Furthermore, Cairncross, Coyle and O'Brien all recognize the possibility that activities will cluster around certain locations for other reasons. Geographic concentration can still produce positive network effects and synergies of co-location: Silicon Valley, for instance, developed alongside the Stanford University campus from which many of its early pioneers were drawn. With the continual churning of labour and spinning off of linked firms, the area has exhibited a considerable gravitational pull for the information technology industries that have grown out of the original, more generalized companies involved in the early development of computers (Fraser 1999: ch. 4). Equally, as I discuss below, Bangalore has emerged as a significant information industry hub in Asia. However, these locations exist not only in physical space, but also, perhaps more importantly, in cyberspace, where the ability of national governments to rule is sharply compromised.

In this new space, authority has been privatized and states are no longer able to govern activities as they did in the past. These globalized networks have broken free from the previous system of state-mediated governance to provide their own authoritative rules (Cutler, Haufler and Porter 1998). Thus, for many commentators, the character of the space in which we live has changed from one defined by governments and their agencies to one which has emerged from the private communications networks set up to serve commercial interests. Activities which take place in spaces previously defined as *within* a particular country may increasingly have causes and implications far from that location, and may be governed by authorities far from where the activity is carried out. Globalization, working with the technologies of the information society, has challenged the previous practices which served to reinforce the notion of national spaces (from border controls to relatively autonomous governments), revealing a new global space: the global information society. This new space is still unevenly developed, with some areas of the world much more linked and integrated than others. Nevertheless, the global information society will slowly (or not so slowly) engulf the world and render the nation-state as a site of authority, and power a thing of the past.

'And Still It Moves'

While aspects of the position I have outlined above are plausible, we should not conclude that the state is no longer of any importance. There is a common but flawed presumption that something called 'globalization' has arrived from *elsewhere* to undermine the state. But states as part of their support for economic development have followed policies that have enhanced globalization. Although largely dependent on technological developments, globalization has been furthered by the 'internationalization' of national economies (promotion of international trade, incentives for foreign investment) and legislative shifts to enhance specific sectors' profitability. Much of this activity has taken place through the imposition of new rules, as well as the reworking of previous (legal) institutions.

Furthermore, arguments regarding the breach of borders through the utilization of new ICTs tend to be myopic, failing to recognize previous waves of technological usage, from the first international postal deliveries, to the telegraph and telephone, which also made borders more transparent. This is not to argue that all is unchanging, or that states are unchallenged by the information age, but rather to suggest that a story of decline simplifies the relationship between states and the (global) information society to such an extent that it presents a severely distorted and inaccurate account of the political economy of the global information society. Even such a seasoned commentator on the emerging new age as Peter Drucker recently admitted: 'Despite all its shortcomings, the nation-state has shown amazing resilience' (1997: 159).

In the last five years political economists have begun to engage with, and modify, the more general claims for the decline of the state in the face of globalization (for instance, Berger and Dore 1996; Hirst and Thompson 1999; Jones 2000; Palan and Abbot 1996; Smith, Solinger and Topik 1999). While I concur with much these authors have to say, here I focus only on claims linked to the proclamation of the information age. I disagree with those who see the information age as signalling the marginalization of the state because they fail to recognize the central role the state has always played in capitalism. And where the state has deployed ICTs to its own advantage, like Phiber Optik they see this not only as a threat to individual liberty but as an attempt to deny the 'real' character of the information age. As I noted in chapter 2, these writers see the internet and its networks as democratic technics, while the authoritarian tendencies of the state are an aberration which is transitional. But the information age encompasses both democratic *and* authoritarian technics; even if we are worried about the ways states and their governments are using ICTs, we need to recognize that states' role in the information age will not automatically decline to reveal a new democratic (Jeffersonian) information society.

Reifying the market and ignoring law

The argument that the state is in decline due to the emergence of the information society conveniently ignores the state's role as guarantor of the legislative infrastructure that underpins market activity. With some exceptions (such as Dyson et al. 1994), arguments stressing decline implicitly accept the 'naturalness' of markets, and fail to acknowledge the importance of property rights to the functioning of normal economic relations. Markets need robust legal arrangements to operate both within and across borders. But if this is forgotten then much necessary state activity is obscured. By removing the state from accounts of the market, the market becomes a natural phenomenon: 'Through reification, the world of institutions appears to merge with the world of nature. It becomes necessity and fate and is lived through as such, happily *or* unhappily as the case may be' (Berger and Luckman 1971: 108). The reification of a naturalized market foregrounds some effects of globalization, and the emergence of an information society, while obscuring the underlying supports on which these developments depend. Globalization and the rise of the information society can then be presented as challenges to the state.

However, the state still plays a crucial role in establishing and enacting the legal form on which information capitalists depend: intellectual property. Furthermore the crucial and central technologies of the information age (ICTs/the internet, biotechnology) were not developed exclusively (or originally) by market actors, but rather stem from major governmental investments in networking and biosciences in the past (Hafner and Lyon 1996; Rifkin 1998). This is not to deny the emergence of various non-state authorities which compete with the state, but to argue that alongside such new authority remains the state's formal positive legal authority, and its ability to support non-commercial economic advances as well as the legal structure required for the smooth operation of capitalist economic relations.

That said, not all states are the same, despite their formal equality as sovereign actors within the international system. Some states have difficulty asserting their formal sovereign independence, but others remain important (indeed indispensable) forces in the information age. Thus Robert Keohane and Joseph Nye suggest that 'one reason that the information revolution has not transformed world politics . . . is that information does not flow in a vacuum but in a political space that is already occupied' (1998: 84). This space is occupied by the state as law-maker, even if not all states are able to successfully maintain such authority. Equally not all states are completely compromised by the tendencies towards deterritorialization and the increasingly porous character of borders: some governments remain able to utilize the agencies and infrastructure of the state to maintain authority through the use of regulatory authority. The often noted unevenness of the global information society is therefore at least partly related to the ability of states to construct a jurisdictional space where their law is recognized and obeyed. Within this jurisdictional space, a particular state's law plays an important role in structuring and shaping social relations. This is because 'law is a moral topography, a mapping of the social world which *normalises* its preferred contours – and, equally importantly, suppresses or at best marginalises other ways of seeing and being' (Corrigan and Sayer 1981: 33). By coding certain outcomes and practices as legal and others not, the state affects certain outcomes and legitimizes coercion against those practices not consistent with such an agenda, although over time this is often subject to negotiation and modification. The state constitutes society through the legal forms it adopts to recognize and legitimize certain activities undertaken by contracting legal individuals.

While the 'information age' does not change the character of capitalism (as I argued in the second chapter), it does require the renewal of certain aspects of property law, most importantly the reconfiguring of intellectual property rights. The information age has prompted the extension of intellectual property into areas previously unavailable for commodification, where such aspects of knowledge and/or information had previously remained in the 'public domain' or the minds of individuals. If capitalism requires new markets to be opened up, the enlarged legal form of intellectual property is necessary for expansion to continue in this direction. We might therefore contend that 'capitalism has not escaped the state, but rather the state has, as always, been a fundamental constitutive element in the very process of extension of capitalism in our time' (Panitch 1996: 109). Without law, societies' economic relations would not appear as they do and these laws in the last analysis are dependent on the authority of the state not only for their formal existence but for the practical ability to rule and shape economic relations.

In the global information society, the laws of intellectual property are 'required' by knowledge capitalists, yet also contested by many social groups. From piracy of copyright through MP3 and its linked software, to campaigns against 'profiteering' in patent-protected AIDS drugs by multinational pharmaceutical companies, intellectual property is riven by disputes regarding its legitimacy and social impact. Here the continuing power and importance of the state stands revealed. Property in the legal sense of 'property amenable to contract' does not pre-exist the apparatus of government (or the state), waiting to be recognized legally; rather the legal recognition of property constitutes its existence in a form that can be identified by economic actors (May 2000a: 16). This is especially the case when it comes to the construction of property in knowledge and information. Only when there is some form of legal apparatus can property be thought of in a way other than merely possession by those with the physical ability to protect themselves from dispossession. More importantly, as there seems to be no 'technological fix' which can make intellectual property robust (successive systems of encryption and/or protection have been 'hacked' or rendered inoperative), the only hope for the protection of such property is law. In this regard, states find themselves mediating through the law the contending interests of capital and its political opponents (as they have done in the past).

And although the institution of property is established enough in modern societies that the sanction of the state to support or enforce this control is seldom needed, behind such acceptance lies the legal strength of the institution. These property rights must be robust as the central requirement of capitalism is the ability to contract for sale (that is, transfer of property) and for work (the labour/employer relation). Without this, the alienation of goods (for sale) and the alienation of labour (to provide capital with work) would be impossible to maintain. Indeed, as Richard Posner suggested to a World Bank Workshop on Legal Reform, 'Legal reform is an important part of the modernization process of poor countries, but the focus of such reform should be on creating substantive and procedurally efficient rules of contract and property rather than on creating a first-class judiciary or an extensive system of civil liberties' (Posner 1998: 9). Posner's clear prioritization of property and contract law over civil liberties indicates again that capitalist market development requires state legislative activity: it is central to the emergence of the 'free' market. Indeed, the emphasis on property rights, law and order and other activities which establish a particular (liberal) market form are now central to the World Bank's development programme typified by its report *The State in a Changing World* (World Bank 1997) and carried forward in its governance programmes.

The state is guarantor of intellectual property and faces no real competitors. This is underlined by the private sector's demands, made more concrete through the Trade Related Aspects of Intellectual Property Rights (TRIPs) agreement under the auspices of the World Trade Organization (WTO), for sufficient protection for their property to be institutionalized through the legal activities of the state. The initial negotiating position of the United States regarding TRIPs was the result of extensive lobbying by a group of twelve MNCs (Drahos 1996: 54; Sell 1998: 137): while MNCs in general may demand less regulation in some areas, intellectual property is not one of them. Rather, at the centre of TRIPs is a radical widening and institutionalization of state authority, from search and seizure based merely on the *suspicion* of infringement, to the introduction of patent laws in sectors (such as pharmaceuticals) where for years developing states have refused protection (May 2000a). For information age entrepreneurs, like all profit-driven market actors, the protection of property is the *sine qua non* of successful activities. Here, as elsewhere, 'global governance requires the nationalisation of international law, which can only be achieved through the reconstitution of sovereignty' (Jayasuriya 1999: 448). The state's role as legislator and police authority is crucial for the continuance of (informational) economic development and the governance of the global information society.

New borders, old borders, old rules, new rules

While the global expansion of ICTs has engendered greater contact between jurisdictions, it also makes explicit what has been the case for some time: 'the allocation of jurisdiction to a particular state is not simply a technical issue; rather, it necessarily involves distributional or political choices' (Trachtman 1998: 569). Thus, specifically (but not exclusively), internet operations can choose (and many have) to take advantage of US law by basing their hubs in the US jurisdiction while their operations are carried out worldwide. Companies may also relocate operations to take advantage of particular national tax regimes. And while this trend is often overstated, the Irish republic has benefited recently from an exodus out of Britain due to new legislation governing e-commerce. Instead of automatically robbing states of the ability to rule and reducing their jurisdiction, ICTs and the information society have continued a trend that has opened up the jurisdictional space to competition, but has also enhanced the possibilities of its expansion (for the most effective states at least).

Although atypical, through its 'effects doctrine' the United States has empowered courts to rule over actions outside US territory which have effects within its borders. Thus on 24 January 2000 the Norwegian Department of Economic Crime arrested Jon Johansen, who had made available on the internet a decryption programme to enable Linux users to play DVDs on their machines. This action broke the US Millennium Copyright Act's rules on the circumnavigation of copy protection systems. While Johansen had committed no offence under Norwegian law, he was indicted on the basis of court proceedings in America (Naughton 2000b). Similarly, the French government recently prosecuted Yahoo for the sale of Nazi memorabilia in internet auctions which it hosts, an action illegal in France. Although the French court required only that such material should not be seen in France (and secured an expert opinion suggesting, despite Yahoo's claims, that this was technically possible), the company has removed the material from its sites altogether, despite being based in the US and not formally subject to French law (Economist 2001: 27). This sort of action is not a possibility for weaker states, but indicates the ability of the US and other major states to expand their effective (or de facto) jurisdiction.

Electronic networks are hardly borderless themselves, although the borders are not necessarily territorial. The imposition (or adoption) of specific sets of technical standards creates default boundaries through which information flows may be more difficult or even impossible (one of the most difficult borders to cross has been the Mac/PC frontier). Such borders exist only electronically but they are reinforced through the regulatory authority that underpins the adoption of specific technical standards. These standards borders are not the same as state borders, but they can be. Technical standards as boundary markers may produce different networked spaces, but states are often able to force such network markers to approximate to state territorial limits. Jamie Metzl suggests this may allow authoritarian governments to continue to oppress and violate human rights with impunity, by using companies' need for protection in this area as a way of controlling communication and content (Metzl 1996: 714–16). This sort of regulatory (re)capture is especially common for satellite broadcasters.

These broadcasters need to ensure that viewers within the satellite footprint pay for their programmes, either by subscription or the purchase of decoders. However, both methods are dependent on the operation of a legal regime for contract relations and the recognition of intellectual property to ensure policing of piracy. Through the ability to render contracts legal and protect (intellectual) property, states can use such protection to retain some level of control and influence over broadcasters. China's ability to encourage Star Channel to drop certain aspects of its news provision, for instance, was largely a result of its ability to support the property rights required by the channel to avoid piracy and unlicensed re-broadcasting. That said, in America, DirecTV has begun to use a software virus (or 'bullet') in its signal that detects and destroys illegal key cards used for receiving transmissions (Lewis 2001). While in this case hackers have been confronted by a technical fix, more often companies rely on the law.

But it is not only in this arena that states continue to maintain regulatory capacity: as Vincent Sica has pointed out, 'states can exploit the same technology that facilitated the globalisation of financial markets to increase their monitoring capacity' (2000: 71). In his study of regulatory activity against money laundering, Sica has established that with the requisite political will, governments can use regulatory apparatus against the immediate interests of financial capital, monitoring and authorizing the 'free' flows of international capital. Even within the financial markets, regarded as paradigmatic of globalization and the effects of widespread utiliza-tion of ICTs, territorial integrity can be reinforced and state author-ity supported. Thus monitoring through licensing and formal regulation remains common, if often dependent on post hoc detec-tion instead of real-time limitation. But 'as anti-money laundering initiatives have become more extensive, they have begun to demon-strate that the new technologies that are said to erode state regula-tory capacity today may in fact even *enhance* it' (Helleiner 1999: 81, emphasis added). Moreover, we should be wary of taking capital flows as exemplary of the character of the global economy.

In the mid-1990s, for the major economies 'more than 80 per cent of production [was] for domestic consumption and more than 80 per cent of investment by domestic investors' (Wade 1996: 61). This is not to deny that cross-border activities are growing but they do not represent the *characteristic* economic interactions of the devel-oped economies. Rather the economic sphere bounded by national borders remains the locus for the majority of all economic activity. And in this sphere, despite the often posited general move towards deregulation, what seems to have occurred is a move to different forms of regulation, a *reregulation* of economic activities (Vogel 1996). Rather than producing an absence of regulation, many recent examples of state-led deregulation have really been regulatory modification and adjustment, with new modes of activity being still regulated, only differently. This may have involved a restructuring of state practices, from revenue raising to industrial support, but it is not indicative of the state becoming less powerful or important.

As Linda Weiss concludes, 'regulatory' activity 'may itself offer states new ways to achieve substantive outcomes, rather than simply to perfect new control procedures' (1999: 82). New rules may serve to push economic activities in particular directions.

Therefore, as Ronen Palan has forcefully argued, the existence of an 'off-shore' sector in the global economy should not be taken as an indication that the state's ability to govern economic relations is declining. It is often assumed that areas where the legal power of the state is subject to a self-denying ordnance indicate that states' governments are struggling to maintain control of economic inter-actions. But 'the right to write the law, which is the essence of sovereign rights, has been interpreted differently in different periods and been used in different ways' (Palan 1998: 630). Although the state may relax its regulation 'off-shore', and although states allow differential regulation within their jurisdiction, such spaces are fundamentally dependent on the state's continuing rule (and are not unregulated, but only *differently* regulated). The provision of 'off-shore' space is one of a number of developmental strategies that may be adopted by particular states. Thus the regulatory space of 'off-shore' exhibits the retention of state authority rather than a nec-essary end to it. Indeed, such spaces could not function without the continuity of some basic laws, not least of all those regulating con-tracts and property rights. Thus, while ICTs may allow companies greater opportunities to manage fragmented operations, and enable them to base some of these operations in Economic Processing Zones (or other 'off-shore' locations), this is not *necessarily* at the cost of the state's ability to regulate and govern such activities.

The presumption that the state power is *inevitably* constrained by ICTs allows any problems linked to the state's (information-related) activities to be ignored or treated as transient. Indeed, while there may be potential for enhancing political freedom through the deployment of ICTs, this is neither inevitable nor necessary: it depends on political will. Where that will is absent or political pres-sures contradict such potentiality, then human rights abusers, dic-tators and oppressors will make use of ICTs, not be halted by them. Here authoritarian technics will triumph over the democratic. In the information age those states able to operate as jurisdictional author-ities will remain important and powerful actors. Those unable to mobilize such authority will see their efficacy challenged, but this is hardly the same as a generalized 'decline of the state', not least of all because those states furthest towards entering the information society are the strongest, not the weakest.

Globalization, the Information Society and the State

Much of the debate and comment about the information age as it relates to states dovetails with claims made about globalization and its effects. But contemporary commentators have been remarkably myopic: actually states (and their governments) still have much to do. In many cases only the state can offer the support that MNCs may find attractive (infrastructure provision, tax holidays and the protection of their property rights). And it is mistaken always to regard competition between states for investment as a 'Dutch auction' or race-to-the-bottom regarding regulatory activity. As I have already noted, for intellectual property rights it is only robust legal protection that is likely to support significant investment. In this regard, India's long resistance to patent protection for pharmaceuticals has been frequently cited by industry groups as the main reason for a lack of multinational development in this industry, although India's own companies have prospered through 'piracy'. For MNCs the real advantages are robust legal structures and the availability of a well-educated, ICT-literate, cheap labour force, another aspect of the economy on which the state has a major impact.

Once we have stepped back from reifying the market, we can see that the legal framework for markets is a key public good not only for the development of capitalism, but also for its continuing health. Dietrich Rueschemeyer and Louis Putterman note: 'The very institutional infrastructure required for functioning markets, as well as developmental state policies, is a prime example of public goods that are beyond the reach of individual market participants' (1992: 247). But this is not the only area where collective action continues to be required: 'many of the public goods a healthy community requires are physical in nature and cannot be provided solely through on-line interaction. Roads, hospitals and schools must be built and maintained and while the Internet can certainly facilitate the production of physical public goods . . . in the end bricks and mortar must be laid' (Kollock 1999: 235). Where market failures reveal the need for (physical) public goods and services (such as education) the state is still required to coordinate the resources (through taxation) for their provision. Thus, while policies to support the development of an information society are sometimes presented as oscillating between neoliberal and dirigiste (Moore 1997), the differences in governmental policy are more in emphasis, over the method of state involvement, rather than whether the state has any role at all. This continuing role has been behind the developmental successes of both India and Ireland.

India, Ireland and information-related development

As I noted in chapter 3, the global information society is starting to change the services which can be relatively easily traded in a global market, opening up new opportunities for state development strategies. For instance, by 1996 India still had only around 1.2 million personal computers (a very low *per capita* rate relative to other major economies), but in the ten years from 1986 its software industry grew from around $10 million to $1.2 billion (Economist 1996). And while this was less than 1 per cent of the entire global market at that time, this rate of increase shows no sign of halting; currently India's software service exports are growing at over 50 per cent a year (Reuters 2000). Significantly, most non-Japanese hardware manufacturers are now outsourcing software development to Indian companies (Dicken 1998: 397). Building on a widespread middle-class use of the English language, and low labour costs, as the Economist succinctly puts it, rather 'than supplying cheap hands . . . India's software companies have prospered by supplying cheap brains' (Economist 1996).

But this is not all India can offer: being ten hours ahead of American Eastern Standard Time means that problems can be solved and jobs undertaken outside the normal working hours in America, especially useful for software maintenance (Wolman and Colamosca 1997: 103–4; Stremlau 1996). Companies ranging from Citibank and American Express to Hewlett Packard and Motorola take advantage of this to ensure around the clock working as well as a reduction in costs. Typically the cost advantage can lead to savings of 50 per cent for software development where work is completely outsourced to Indian contractors, while this falls when work is shared between sites (Heeks et al. 2000). Although not all global outsourcing relationships involving Indian software firms have been successful, the sector is steadily growing and becoming more significant for the Bangalore region's continuing economic development.

This booming information economic sector has transformed Bangalore itself, leading to further investment and development. This is no accident: the government-owned software developer and exporter, Infosys, is based there, as is Silicon Graphics (whose location was influenced by state support), while local provision of training and education for information technology professionals continues to be expanded. There is also a booming private training sector, offering courses to prospective call-centre workers and other information operatives. This success is starting to reverse the 'brain drain' which affected India in the past, with many professionals returning to set up their own companies or work for established service providers (Wolman and Colamosca 1997: 99). The ability to reverse the flow of the 'best minds' is no small achievement and is mirrored in the Irish experience.

The economic boom of the last ten years has required the Republic of Ireland's state training agency to reorient its activities. Whereas in the past the agency helped Irish expatriates to find work in foreign cities (such as Berlin or Paris), it now runs Jobs Ireland a worldwide recruitment drive intended to encourage workers to come (or return) to Ireland. With Europe's fastest growing economy, the Irish need more and more workers (many in the lower-level service jobs natives no longer want, but also in the professions), requiring the government to enact a three-fold expansion of non-EU work permits in 2000 (Economist 2000f). And although Ireland's workforce is often cited as a reason for relocation, the government has also moved to enhance its education system to raise the skills of its domestic labour pool (Hirst 2000). Importantly, the Irish government has maintained and expanded its Industrial Development Agency to encourage inward investment by information-related companies, in stark contrast to the problems experienced with the underfunded and weak regional development agencies across the Irish Sea.

For companies located in Ireland, the country not only offers a relatively light tax burden but also provides a panoply of investment and employment supports (Hirst 2000). As well as regulatory activity to support economic growth, the Irish government has undertaken more focused infrastructure activities to support information-related enterprise. Building on its legacy of cable TV provision, Ireland already has 80 per cent domestic connectivity, and is developing widespread broadband access well ahead of its neighbours in Europe. It is the landing point for a major transatlantic cable link putting it at the centre of a global network connecting America to Europe, and the Irish government has underwritten the purchase of guaranteed capacity on this link for Irish companies and users (Brown 2000). Finally, the Irish government has been careful not to regulate in a manner which will preclude or deter information-related investments, unlike the British government (most recently with the Regulation of Investigatory Powers, or RIP, bill). And similarly, although more quietly, and spearheaded by Nokia, the Finnish (in the words of Castells) have become 'the first true information society', with almost comprehensive availability of information services and infrastructural support (Castells 2000: 78). Certainly the states in these countries do not seem to have been marginalized.

Individual rights and democracy in the information age

As I have mentioned, much of the commentary on the information society presents it as 'naturally' democratic: the deployment and widespread use of ICTs will enhance the associative possibilities of society and engender new communities in civil society. If the state figures in these commentaries, it is conceived of as a threat. However, the state still has an important role to play in maintaining democracy in the information society. Neil Netanel suggests that a lack of state authority in cyberspace will 'free majorities to trample upon minorities' while allowing 'invidious status discrimination, narrowcasting and mainstreaming content selection, systematic invasions of privacy and gross inequalities in the distribution of basic requisites for netizenship [sic] and citizenship' (2000: 498). Only the state, for instance through the legal support for privacy rights, and legislating against discrimination, can ensure the information age remains democratic in a meaningful manner. Although perhaps a pessimistic view of human nature, nevertheless history has seen major advances in minority and individual rights *only* when states have legislated for them. Rights to equal treatment must, if they are to be robust, be legal rights. Indeed, without legislation, any protection is contingent, based on favour or personal power, and such protection does not amount to 'rights': rights require law.

Furthermore, different groups will have different (or even opposed) views about what rights need to be supported, as well as more general concerns about the character and effects of regulation. Debates about these issues need to take place in public if they are to reflect democratic values of equality and justice. This public space in which such mediation, deliberation and negotiation can be facilitated needs to be supported by an accountable state, so all views can be properly considered without prejudice (Noveck 2000). But while governments in most rich countries (and some not so rich) are developing their ICT-related capacities, in the main this has revolved around the construction of communication pathways to elicit the information the state needs to govern (electronic information submission to tax authorities and other governmental agencies, for instance) or the publication of reports and draft legislation online. This is not the same as opening up deliberative processes to public participation. Rather, the deployment of ICTs is often 'designed to make government service delivery more effective or more "customer oriented" . . . [and does] no more than respond to a general demand from citizens for government institutions to be cost-effective and efficient' (Tops, Horrocks and Hoff 2000: 179). Despite the emergence of some localized ICT-mediated deliberative forums, central governments have yet to move far in the direction of information age democracy.

However, in their overview of research into the political potential of ICTs, Pieter Tops and his colleagues also suggest that the democratic renewal of state and governmental decision-making is at least possible. This remains spasmodic and underdeveloped because 'the desire to realise more efficient government performance, together with the design of new information systems, often provokes a kind of "techno-utopian" discourse which is guided by the technocratic ideals of rational decision-making' (Tops, Horrocks and Hoff et al. 2000: 180). Thus, on the one hand, governments seldom seem interested in enhancing the ability of citizens to engage with the democratic process as anything more than receivers of information or services. In this sense the rule of the technocrats, proposed by Daniel Bell a quarter of a century ago, retains a certain salience for governments. On the other hand, the state remains the clearest legitimate authority that has the (legal) ability to enforce its decisions and regulations where rights are concerned, thus remaining the most likely agent for the construction of a democratically inclined information society (Netanel 2000: 486–8 and *passim*). For (intellectual) property rights the role of the state is taken as self-evident, and I see little reason to expect that individual rights will be respected without similar recourse to legal support.

However, the position of governments remains ambiguous at best, as the debates over privacy and surveillance indicate. Here the state represents both the most obvious legislator to protect rights to privacy, and also, as the recent machinations of the British government have shown, a significant threat. As Paul Schwartz contends, once linked to the internet, 'the computer on our desk becomes a potential recorder and betrayer of our confidences' (1999: 1611). Schwartz himself sees this development as initiating a 'privacy horror show'. Certainly, the 'clipper chip' reflected the US government's wish to retain the key to encryption technologies that were being sold both in America and for export, to facilitate state agencies' access to any 'suspect' communications. More recently, the British government's RIP bill has legalized the enhanced capacity the intelligence services 'need' to continue to collect vital (security sensitive) information from private communications. In their bid to control the emergence of 'virtual crime' and the criminal use of ICT-mediated networks, individual privacy (unfortunately, we are told) must be sacrificed.

By ignoring the continuing capacity of the state, much discussion of the information age fails fully to appreciate the importance of the relationship between state and citizen. Furthermore, having been told repeatedly that the state is in decline, or outmoded, many users may fail to perceive the impact governmental actions could have on them. When the state's role in the information age is ignored or downplayed, governments are left a freer hand to indulge in the sorts of actions which should be held more democratically accountable than they are. Where there is the possibility of surveillance, political communication may be circumscribed (as in many authoritarian states) or at least driven underground. In Britain and America such actions can be made subject to some sort of debate (which is not to say they will). Disappointingly, despite considerable media attention, the RIP bill's threat to privacy has not engendered widespread political concern (Naughton 2000c). This may be because there is actually popular support for some forms of surveillance (of recidivist criminals, especially sex criminals, for instance), though this may also lead to the rights of minorities being disregarded.

This raises the problem of the tyranny of the majority and the ability to establish universal rights in democracies. Charles Raab argues that the key role of the state in the information age is to provide for the discussion and adoption of open and effective rules for the treatment of personal (and non-personal) information (1995: 210–11). Where these rules do not exist, individuals may be reluctant to engage in anything more than routine communication through ICTs, slowing the very development towards an information society the anti-statists proclaim. The role of the state must therefore balance the need for privacy with the legitimate needs of the general citizenry to know who is who and what is what. In other words, 'information privacy rules must evaluate the demands for personal data along with the need for restrictions on access that will encourage speech' (Schwartz 1999: 1652). Only an accountable democratic authority can conduct such a balance fairly, and even then British (and American) intelligence community initiatives suggest this may need to be carefully scrutinized by citizens and their representatives. Such oversight, however, is frequently diffi-cult to establish, especially where governments deny the existence of the systems over which scrutiny is sought (most recently the ECHELON communications interception system).

Nevertheless, if democracy needs open communication but also the protection of oppositional discourse from censure (legalized or popular), then only the state is in a position to support such a demo-cratic space. Certainly market solutions cannot be depended on to protect minority rights, especially in areas like privacy (Lessig 1999: 163). Even where guarantees of privacy have been given, there have already been cases of information being sold on in one form or another, directly violating the intent (if not always the exact wording) of such guarantees. While it may seem an anathema to some to trust any government over privacy, at least (some) gov-ernments remain formally accountable. Private provision of privacy 'rights' would be subject to the vagaries of the market, expediency and a lack of potential legal recourse. However, despite these demo-cratic arguments for a substantive involvement of state agencies in the furtherance of individual rights, the only area where state agen-cies have explored the full potentiality of ICTs is in the realm of security and defence.

The state and information warfare

The American 'military-industrial complex' has always played a significant role in the support of high-tech research and was a major factor in the origins of the internet. Thus it is hardly surprising that the one area of state competency in the information age which has garnered considerable attention is information warfare (see, for instance, Adams 1998; Arquilla and Rondfelt 1997; Schwartzstein 1996). The 'information revolution' in the security forces is the most recent Revolution in Military Affairs (RMA). Previous revolutions (from the invention of the bow, through the development of rifles, tanks and aeroplanes, to the utilization of nuclear weapons) have changed the ways wars have been fought and the manner in which countries have defended themselves. Methods of warfare and perceived threats to the state have once again been 'revolutionized' by the widespread deployment and use of ICTs. New technologies may allow invaders or in-country groups to mobilize more swiftly, attacking through well-informed campaigns that target weak spots. But, equally, weapons systems are becoming 'smarter', leading to a transformation of the risks to the lives of the fighting forces of information-adept armies.

Overall, information war (the disruption of informational links utilizing aggressive software) may make the state more susceptible to security threats even as it upgrades its defence technologies. In 2000 President Clinton proposed a $2 billion fund to develop and deploy countermeasures in this area, in the wake of high-profile 'attacks' by an Israeli teenager and by Russian intelligence operatives on the Pentagon computer system (Borger 2000a). Elsewhere, China and Taiwan have conducted information warfare against each other: Chinese agents targeted economic communications, prompting the Taiwanese authorities to hit back by hacking into the website of China's tax authorities and the railways ministry (Economist 1999b). Sophisticated 'firewalls' to guard information capabilities are always incomplete (to allow usage by legitimate users) and can be breached by 'Trojan horse' software programs, making such attacks a constant concern. The more such technologies are utilized, and therefore the more widely spread the information networks used, the more potentially vulnerable defence systems become.

Attacks are not limited to government sites, but also may be aimed at commercial sites, as the 'denial of service' problems in February 2000 encountered by Yahoo, Amazon and eBay, among others, illustrated. Launched from multiple (unknowing, hence 'zombie') sites, these attacks from anti-capitalist demonstrators led to demands for the US authorities to step in and prosecute the offending hackers. More recently, similar attacks on Microsoft prompted the company to call in the FBI. This usefully illustrates a paradox at the centre of the debate about the relevance of the state in the information age: information economy practitioners argue that 'e-commerce must be free and unregulated. The Internet should not be taxed . . . The less government there is in cyberspace, the better. But guess what – when their systems are cracked, the ideologues who mouth these mantras are the first to run screaming to the government for help' (Naughton 2000a). By virtue of the internet's global reach, the American authorities may have some difficulty bringing to court the hackers who have launched these and other attacks (not least of all as it is not always clear what the charges might be), but as I noted above, the US courts can and have claimed extraterritorial jurisdiction in certain cases. If these threats are regarded as being matters of national security then such extraterritoriality will again be asserted. More importantly, when attacked the state suddenly seems a little less irrelevant to the beneficiaries of the information age.

State agencies treat these threats to information security not so much as direct threats from identifiable groups, but as 'something more akin to disease', something to continually guard against (Libicki 1998: 427). Security has become more systemic; threats are not necessarily going to be related to other states. Developed states are therefore keen to use ICTs to heighten their awareness of such threats: hence the British and American governments interest in accessing all electronic communications when national security seems threatened (by political groups or criminals). Mobile phones especially, but also email, allow groups to organize without expensive investments in communications systems; information availability has been widened, allowing antagonists many of the strategic advantages previously limited to well-resourced national armies, such as access to satellite photographs of targeted areas and installations (Dehqanzada and Florini 2000). The emergence of a new sort of conflict, where the state is joined by other actors to combine 'warfare' with elements of organized crime and terrorism, is therefore reinforced by ICTs. New security threats are increasingly pluralized, private and public, local and global (Kaldor 1999). Information technology enables diverse actors to come together in the pursuit of particular goals through violence and to melt away when the state is too powerful or when success has been achieved. These are the new threats which have become the central concern of military planners.

On the one hand, the state is an unwieldy organization which may be vulnerable to the small-scale operations which can have quite devastating consequences for the information infrastructure, as well as to life and limb. But, on the other, the state is still able to mobilize significant resources to conduct information war, and utilize information to improve the targeting of security service operations. The use of intelligence resources can be made more efficient by deploying powerful ICTs, allowing a much greater ability to coordinate (quickly) diverse intelligence sources. The state's intelligence resources far outstrip those of groups who threaten it, and ICTs can increase this advantage. Furthermore, the RMA enhances the most technically adept forces: the ability to deploy information resources and ICT-equipped armaments makes war with few human costs (on one's own side, at least) possible. Whatever else we might say about the Gulf War, the technical superiority of the American and NATO equipment was clearly demonstrated, not least of all by the disproportionate casualties on the opposing side.

However, war itself will remain similar (in effects at least) to previous conflicts between states and other armed groups. Responding to claims that cyberwar is profoundly different, Colin Gray points out that this is not the first time an RMA has suggested that war will be transformed, and in the past such transformations have been less far-reaching than expected. He suggests that reading today's accounts of cyberwar 'is, in a sense, to read the texts of yesterday's prophets for air power and armoured and mechanised ground forces' (Gray 1996: 276). War is still about the destruction of an enemy's resources for battle (whatever they may be), and in the final analysis will involve the loss of life. Or, as Lawrence Freedman concludes, the RMA 'does not offer the prospect of a virtual war by creating a situation in which only information matters so that there is never any point in fighting about anything other than information . . . War is not a virtual thing, played out on screens, but intensely physical. That is why it tends towards violence and destruction' (1998: 78). Which is to say that, despite the information society, war will remain a violent and bloody affair based on the competition for physical resources and power, but the deployment of ICTs can skewer the costs of the conflict onto the other (less ICT-adept) side. However, 'even with precise information, it is necessary to strike and destroy the target' (Gouré 1996: 227). The threat of information war may be a new threat which states need to factor into their considerations, but it does not replace the need to maintain a defensive capability to deal with conventional attacks.

Technological superiority will 'mean little without organizational superiority', without which 'superior weapons have only a tactical significance' (Blank 1997: 70). Thus, while an information warfare attack may take the state by surprise or render it temporarily vulnerable, the ability to organize a complex and comprehensive response is more likely to lie with the state than the individual or the virtual community under attack – hence the response of companies to the 'denial of service' onslaught. A key element of (information) warfare is the ability to 'illuminate the battlefield' (Libicki 1998). On one level this concerns the ability to track the movements of the enemy better than it can see yours. But it also, and importantly, includes the ability to follow the traces that computer activities leave (and on which the surveillance possibilities of ICTs are based). This means that while the initial advantage may lie with the aggressor, the chance to escape detection is largely illusory. Even those who propose information war as the future of conflict regard the state as playing a major role in equipping society to deal with this new threat. These new threats may spur a reassessment of responses, but they do not indicate the state's withdrawal from security.

A Death Frequently Foretold

The debate about the decline of the state questions where effective sovereignty will lie in the information age and also suggests that the importance of physical space, of particular locations, has been undermined. Some commentators imply that the technologies of the information age have relieved many of the inefficiencies of society which previously rendered the apparatus of the state necessary, and thus that the state no longer fulfils a useful function. However, as I have been arguing throughout this book, the power relations of capitalism remain largely undisturbed by the information society and therefore any supposed expansion in the empowerment of the citizenry is largely illusory. Conversely, the state itself is still able to mobilize extensive informational resources, and has always been a major user, producer and supplier of information. While its other resources (from military power to tax receipts) may be adversely affected by the information age, as I have explored above, the state still retains extensive areas of competency, crucial for the emergence and development of the information society. If this is so, then the claim that we are experiencing the 'end of geography' is, at the very least, premature.

Nevertheless, there is the possibility of a widespread reconfiguration of the advantages offered by specific locations. States' governments have a potentially significant role in adapting to the 'new' demands of the information age; governmental actions may significantly enhance the advantages enjoyed by specific locations in the information economy. Additionally, the importance of less tangible locational advantages may expand, not least of all the attractiveness of particular social settings. Joel Kotkin argues that in the new geography 'the important distinctions between locations, and the variables governing their success, have become, if anything, *more* important' (2000: 7, emphasis in original). As with other technological changes, perhaps most significantly the advent of cheap automobiles, there will be shifts in the advantages (social, political and economic) offered by particular locations. However, this is not the same as a decline in the importance of differences. Rather, the claim that space itself has changed is ideologically charged.

Thinking about how we conceive of the spaces in which our social relations take place, Henri Lefebvre suggested: 'we may be sure that representations of space have practical impact, that they intervene in and modify spatial *textures* which are informed by effective knowledge and ideology' (1991: 42). The claim that the physical space in which states exist is somehow being marginalized or at least declining in importance is a crucial element of the 'Californian ideology'; states (and their governments) have been sidelined. State-oriented politics are largely obsolete because they operate in a space which is no longer so important. Moreover the space which is becoming important precludes effective state activity. The representation of 'cyberspace' is meant to indicate that we should no longer look to the state for an effective political response. However, given the continuing activities of the states in a number of areas, this claim is more driven by a wish to see the state marginalized in certain but not all areas of its activity (the desire for small government) than by any assessment of what states actually do.

Sidelining the state means that the ability to hold governments accountable for their continued important regulatory activities is not only underdeveloped, but often wilfully ignored or regarded as anachronistic. Certainly, agencies like the World Bank still see a major role for the state in the information age (World Bank 1997: *passim*; 1999: 144–56), but many commentators on information society seem reluctant to recognize this continuity. Thus Boris Frankel's conclusion about the utopian wishes regarding the state remains as prescient as it was fifteen years ago:

> Either one aims for a stateless society – possibly organized around 'basic communes' – and argues for the feasibility of this post-

industrial utopia; or else, one is forced to recognize that state institutions are not mere political-administrative apparatuses . . . and will
continue to be heavily involved in the many social relations normally
defined as belonging to 'civil society'. (1987: 203)

If we regard the former as unrealistic (or implausible), then the politics of the information age are not about getting rid of the state but
rather deciding how states and their governments can help facilitate and deliver the sort of society we want. It all 'depends on how
people think about stateness' (Evans 1997: 87). We need to recognize that states have a continuing and profoundly important role to
play, especially in the face of the technological changes ushered in
by the information age.

   And while I have mainly focused on the legal role the state plays
in the information age, I could also have looked at the continuing
role of the postindustrial welfare state (Esping-Andersen 1999) or
spent more time examining its developmental capacities (Palan and
Abbot 1996; Weiss 1998). Furthermore, the infrastructure (most significantly high-speed cable connections) that the information
society's networks depend on is hardly universally accessible. This
is not only a problem for developing states struggling to join the
information society, but can be a regional problem in developed
states. In Britain 'high upfront investment costs, sparse populations
and a less affluent consumer base will soon make rural roll-out of
some technologies commercially unviable. In theory, the Internet
connects dispersed people. In practice, it is highlighting divisions
. . . Britain's technological atlas is fragmented and highly fluid. But
the dearth of rural services is constant' (Grande 2000). If the
problems of high-level services being offered only in densely pop-
ulated locations is already evident in Britain, we can imagine the
greater distinctions in connectivity between rural and urban areas
in poorer countries (where even more basic services and technologies may be beyond the incomes of prospective users). Certainly commercial considerations will do little to alleviate this
problem, leaving the state to deal with those disadvantaged by
these discrepancies.

   Overall, despite the proclamations that the state is in decline
because of the changing political and economic character of the
information age, many celebrants of the information society completely misunderstand what the state does. Only by understanding
the continuing role of states and their governments can the information society become (or remain) democratic, because without rec-

ognizing how much the state does, how can it be held accountable? In some ways state actions may be in tension with the potentiality of the information age, but equally in many ways such potentiality depends on the state to support and enact its legal underpinnings and social structures.

6

Back to the Future

There have been many changes we might link to the development of new information and communication technologies (ICTs).
However, there is also much about the global information society
which is similar to previous modes of social interaction: economics
is still recognizable as modern (or perhaps late) capitalism; despite
forecasts of increased 'virtualization', politics, communities and
other aspects of social existence remain located in the material
world; states continue to play an active and important role in our
lives. Thus there is no need to discard all previous analyses and
insight, no need to dispense with our previous 'ideological
baggage'. Indeed, the claim that we *should* is ideological in itself. It
represents a dismissal of well-developed arguments regarding the
contested and contingent character of capitalism, while also presenting a specific set of contemporary social relations as natural and
outside history. But, Krishan Kumar points out,

> To call the information society an ideology and to relate that ideol-
> ogy to the contemporary needs of capitalism is to begin, not end the
> analysis. Capitalism has had many ideologies over the past two-
> hundred years – *laissez-faire*, managerialism, welfarism . . . Each has
> had its own kind of relation to capitalist society; each has contained
> its own distinctive contradictions. (1995: 34)

Or, as Carolyn Marvin once remarked, 'Information age rhetoric is
the start-fresh propaganda of our age' (1987: 61). Information
society commentary is often suffused with technological determin-

ism (naturalizing the thrust of technology). It disavows our role in applying the technologies that are available to us, and denies the social shaping of technology.

These new technologies do not represent neutral mechanisms, or novel developments lacking histories, but rather are a technological manifestation of the historically specific social system in which they have emerged. But although it obscures much, the notion of information society is not completely without foundation: there have been changes, though not as great in magnitude as supposed, nor necessarily in the directions forecast. Where there have been significant changes in technological deployment and use these have left the substance of social relations either untouched, or little altered. At the beginning of this book I suggested that the distinction between changes in form and a continuity in substance was a helpful shorthand for the argument I wanted to make. Throughout the subsequent chapters the underlying theme has been this contradiction between claims for (revolutionary) change and the evident continuities in society. But these contradictions have also revealed sites of potential contestation and mediation for those who remain sceptical about the utopian forecasts of a benign global information society.

Shortcomings of Technological Forecasting

Fantasies and fears about technological advances in society are hardly unprecedented. Innovations in information technology, from writing to computers, have always engendered speculation regarding their impact on social organization. In the fifth century BC, Plato reported that Socrates regarded writing as dangerous, because it would lead memory to decline, would be used for cataloguing rather than understanding, would increase problems of authentication of knowledge, and was only a shadow of oral rhetoric. Socrates believed writing would fatally compromise the previous organization of Greek society, maintained through oral interaction (Everard 2000: 122). While some of these concerns may have been apposite, it is difficult to conceive of a modern society without the ability to communicate through written media. Indeed, Albertine Gaur has argued that without writing to record and mark property, economic development towards societies based on market exchange would have been impossible (Gaur 1992: 16–17, 23). Throughout the history of technology, some have hoped particular technological advances would bring us nearer to a specific utopia, while others have feared the same new technology would bring disaster and social collapse.

The warnings of a disaster of gargantuan proportions at the end of 1999 (the so-called Y2K problem) were a contemporary, and widely reported, example of such doom-laden technological prediction. Due to the early use of two-digit year systems in software (such as '99' instead of '1999') the roll over to 2000 would, we were told, confuse many numerically driven devices, making the new year look like 1900 not 2000. This would cause massive and extensive systems failure prompting a general social meltdown (Anson 1998). Survivalists started hoarding food and arms in expectation of widespread anarchy, while stories suggesting that planes would fall from the sky and nuclear reactors would run critical were widely reported. As it was, nothing of the sort came to pass; we all went out and enjoyed ourselves, waking up the next morning to spasmodic reports of small-scale problems that normally would not have warranted any attention in the news media.

This reveals some important problems with forecasting. First, publicizing the forecast itself may amend and change behaviour. This may be intentional or alternatively used as an excuse for the predicted circumstance failing to appear. Thus, in the new year we were reassured that the impact of the Y2K problem was minimized by widespread upgrading and software engineering work prior to the night of 31 December 1999. Conversely, the forecasts of the information society have been intended to encourage the social developments they purported to 'recognize'. Secondly, technological predictions have a tendency to overemphasize the centrality of the technology concerned in our lives. Thus, although there were some problems associated with the turn of the millennium, these did not spread out in a swift geometric expansion as some doomsayers predicted. Moreover, countries and companies that had spent little were hardly more affected than those that had devoted considerable resources to 'solving' the problem. Like many ICT-related predictions, the Y2K problem was less significant than expected. Information society forecasts forget that ICTs are one (albeit powerful) technology among many and that humans do not completely depend on technology in all (or even most) areas of social existence.

There is also a third, less immediately obvious lacuna in technological predictions: the lack of foresight regarding effects that seem important in hindsight. While hindsight is always 20:20 vision there is often a glaring inconsistency between forecasts and outcomes. For example, one problem which has been almost completely missed by commentators on information society is how we dispose of millions of obsolete computers. Loaded with toxic substances (cadmium, mercury, dioxins and lead), over a million PCs are going into landfills every year, but this is hardly a sustainable method of disposal (Sweet 2000). It is an environmental problem which is expanding (and becoming more dangerous) every day but which was not predicted, or even mentioned, in any account of the emergence of an information society I have read. Not all predictions are proved wrong because they overstate the possible effects of a particular technology: aspects of their impact may only become apparent in retrospect.

Early forecasts for information technology had little idea of the likely impact of computing. As Paul Ceruzzi points out, because early computers were so cumbersome, and used only for highly specialized mathematical work, there was little reason to expect their use to become more widespread. He argues that 'three factors contributed to the erroneous picture of the computer's future: a mistaken feeling that computers were fragile and unreliable; the institutional biases of those who shaped policy towards computer use in the early days; and an almost universal failure, even among the computer pioneers themselves, to understand the very nature of computing' (Ceruzzi 1997: 120). With faster and smaller machines, the expansion of hobby and home use, and the realization of the capacity for information processing that computers brought, early predictions of limited utility were revealed as hopelessly mistaken about the future of computer use. Unable to see the way social use might develop as the technology improved, the expected trajectory of these early accounts missed the possibilities for home and office PCs (personal computers) completely, and supposed that computers would always be large centralized, service-specific machines.

But we should not be too judgmental; it may be difficult to understand the effects of technology even *after* the fact. Discussing the impact of the telephone after nearly a century, Ithiel de Sola Pool noted that it was 'not much easier to answer the "what if" questions of history than the "what if" questions about the future' (de Sola Pool 1998: 186). Attempts at counterfactual history (how would modern cities have evolved without the telephone or the automobile, for instance?) are no easier than predicting the future. This might indicate that we should be cautious in our forecasts for the social effects of new technologies, but (as we have seen) little prudence has been evident in the discussion of the prospects for the global information society in the new millennium. In the last twenty-five years the predicted impact of ICTs has not been down-played or even moderated; rather it has became exaggerated and universalized.

Incremental improvement or revolution

Forecasts of the importance of certain technologies seem to lack an appreciation that not all new technologies have the same scale of impact. Reflecting these differences we might divide technological advances or innovations into two groups, which Peter Golding calls 'Technology One' and 'Technology Two': 'Technology One allows existing social action and process to occur more speedily, more efficiently, or conveniently (though equally possibly, with negative consequences, such as pollution and risk). Technology Two enables wholly new forms of activity previously impracticable or even inconceivable' (2000: 171). Problems for prediction and forecasting arise when Technology One is mistakenly identified as Technology Two. In the debates around information society this is a frequent and far-reaching cause of exaggeration of the effects of the information age. If ICTs are a Technology One, then it is unsurprising that the changes they have prompted have been less than revolutionary – indeed this would be expected. But if ICTs are (mistakenly) seen as a Technology Two, then this lack of a manifest revolutionary effect requires the identification of a truly transformative information age to be constantly presented as a forthcoming development, as it frequently is.

Unlike other technical forecasts, in the last twenty years predictions of the expanding technical capacity of microchips (their processing velocity, or clockspeed), and concomitant reductions in price, have proved remarkably accurate. However, due to the confusion regarding Technologies One and Two, this important but quantitative change has led to qualitative arguments regarding the effects on society. Thus, recently, it has been suggested that telemedicine (access to doctors over the internet) will in the future come to be regarded as revolutionary an innovation as the introduction of antibiotics proved to be (see Dillon 2001). This confuses an improvement in speed and style of communication (after all we can already phone our doctors) with a shift in medical possibilities (as antibiotics surely were). A better contender in this field for Technology Two status is biotechnology, which while certainly supported by the deployment of ICTs, is separate from them. The claim that biotechnology allows 'wholly new forms of activity previously impracticable or even inconceivable' is much more plausible. While biotechnology seems to allow new and revolutionary uses or applications with profound social implications, ICTs are generally applied to already existing social practices, and therefore their use is more likely to 'improve' current practices, not stimulate new social organization.

Nevertheless, the key issue for forecasting is not the technologies themselves but how they are applied. At the height of the second wave of commentary on the information society, Steven Schnaars warned against commentators being captured by 'technological wonder' (1989: 143–4). Technological wonder at the capabilities in the underlying technologies blinds forecasters to the relative continuity in the practices to which they are applied. That said, wonder can fade: recently Bill Gates admitted that providing computers to the poor in developing countries might not be the best way forward for improving living conditions. He asked: 'Do people have a clear view of what it means to live on a $1 a day? . . . There's no electricity in that house. None . . . The mothers are going to walk right up to that computer and say "My children are dying, what can you do?" They're not going to sit there and browse eBay' (quoted in Martinson 2000). This has led Gates himself to concentrate on healthcare in his philanthropic giving, prompting the conclusion that 'computers are amazing in what they can do, but they *have to be put into the perspective of human values*' (quoted in Helmore and McKie 2000, emphasis added). Although derided for these remarks by industry figures who maintain a tranformative vision of the information society, Gates seems to have finally recognized that ICTs, which his company has done so much to promote, can only be regarded as *part* of human existence, not as defining its character.

Technological wonder also reflects technological determinism, the idea that new technologies drive historical and social changes (which I discussed in chapter 2). But there is an alternative view, summed up by Doreen Massey: 'New technology is created; and it is a social creation. Our responsibilities do not lie solely in mitigating its effects, in adapting society to its demands and implications. There is social choice also, and a social responsibility, for the very nature of new technology' (1985: 312). Technology has no independent existence outside the society in which it is developed, indeed it is a product of that society and reflects the character, mores and interests of that society. New technologies are deployed in ongoing social relations and although they may impact on those relations, such effects are not necessarily revolutionary or socially transforming. The impact of technology is not unmediated or automatic; it is the subject of social negotiation, reflecting previous social settlements and practices.

One further problem with much of the celebratory writing I have examined should be mentioned: it is often based on the universalization of a writer's own experiences. Charles Leadbeater, William Mitchell, Esther Dyson, Nicholas Negroponte, Charles Handy, Alvin Toffler and numerous others have looked at their own lives and assumed this is the model for the future. Although they have successfully developed 'portfolio careers', responding to perceived shifts in the way capitalists manage knowledge, their experience is not as common as they think. They move in relatively closed groups of like-minded and similarly employed people and have been insulated from the real world of service work, contingent employment and surveillance. They frequently advise companies and agencies closely associated with the deployment of new ICTs. And therefore their access to the coming world of the information society is mediated by that world's promoters, which means that their predictions are hardly disinterested. For these writers the technological possibilities from which they have benefited are universally available (or in less extreme moments, potentially universal) and therefore their life choices will be available to everyone. This universalizing myopia stems from a particular view about the 'natural' character of the information age, which they arrogantly presume is encapsulated in their own experiences.

The Dual Dynamic of Information Society

As I suggested in chapter 2, too often the character of the information society is regarded either as naturally democratic/disclosing *or* authoritarian/enclosing, whereas it is, much more plausibly, both. Lewis Mumford suggested that the dialectical relationship between democratic and authoritarian technics is the underlying story of the history of technology. There is no compelling need to regard the information age as any different; no need to place it outside the continuing history of technology's interaction with society. After all, the history of technology *is* the history of technological innovation and its social impact. Recognizing the dual dynamic of technological history enables us to see why there has been a lack of revolutionary change in the global information society, despite an almost constant expectation of transformation. In each of the three areas I have examined (labour and property; community and politics; the role of the state) the possibilities of democratic technics have been compromised and minimized by authoritarian technics. But conversely, the effects of authoritarian technics have been ameliorated and lessened by the potential for, and development of, democratic technics. Unfortunately this interplay is frequently unobserved, discounted, or regarded as merely transitory.

Taking work and the relations between labour and capital first, the twin dynamics are clear. On the one side, ICTs have allowed many (knowledge) workers better work conditions and may enhance their ability to control the means of production now that these 'means' are located in their minds. Claims about the future of work and the social benefits of new information (service) occupations reflect a real and existing democratic technics which has clearly benefited certain groups of workers. However, such optimism needs to be tempered by recognizing the ability of capitalists (employers) to retain significant control through the use of ICTs, most obviously through the potential for surveillance and direction/formalization of work. Furthermore, the expansion in the use of various forms of intellectual property has done little to empower knowledge workers overall. Rather, in the majority of cases it has allowed the continuation of the 'normal' social relations of capitalism, the ownership of labour's (intellectual) output by capitalists. The enclosing (authoritarian) dynamic has frequently slowed, and almost halted, the developments in working relationships which the disclosing perspective (stressing democratic technics) regards as characteristic of the emerging information age. But it has not completely closed off the potential of democratic technics; only made it something that needs to be struggled for, rather than expected as a 'natural' progression.

Similarly, when I discussed (new) communities and politics in the information age, there were some indications of a democratic or disclosing potential to ICTs and their social deployment. This is stimulating new forms of political activity, while also engendering new developments in the organization of more usual forms of politics. Campaigns have utilized the internet, email and mobile phones to stage 'just-in-time' demonstrations that have proved difficult for state authorities to contain. Furthermore, there is a growing interest in treating the world as a global civil and political society which has been greatly enhanced by interactivity. Information about humans rights abuses, environmental degradation, slavery and other social problems is much harder to restrict or censor. This has opened up a space for political organizations to try and change state and private sector behaviour either directly (in democracies) or indirectly (diplomatic pressure channelled through the state system). But, once again, there has been a contrary dynamic compromising these shifts.

Authoritarian technics have manifested themselves both in the continuity of previous social status in 'new' communities and in barriers to communicative interaction, but also in the continuing lack of a viable public domain on the internet (where it might have been expected to emerge). Indeed, despite the new possibilities for interaction, political engagement does not seem to be growing, there is no mass expansion of participatory democracy (at least partly due to wealth effects), nor (yet) a *mass* movement based round global, or information-related, issues. This is evident when citizens are not exercising the (supposedly) expanded potential for political activity, but also when governments fail to provide avenues for ICT-mediated participatory democracy.

This brings us to the third area: the role of the state. Democratic technics might imply that the state would be in decline, with power increasingly localized and distant state authority and regulation becoming outmoded. Some states have certainly been threatened by groups using ICTs, from China's problems with the Falun Gong to the British government's conflict with protesters at the price of fuel. But states and their governments (reflecting authoritarian technics) retain much of their power and authority, though ICTs may have changed the way this is mobilized. Indeed, the rule of law, and with it the authority of the state, is ever more important where knowledge and information (the key resources of the information age) need to be treated as property.

Lewis Mumford recognized that these two dynamics are not contradictory. The move to control and enclosure (authoritarian technics in their systemic mode) exists alongside the tendency to disclosure (the possibility and potential of democratic technics). For Mumford the history of technology was a process of interaction and conflict between democratic and authoritarian technics, a dialectic. It is crucial to recall that technics are not the result of *specific* technologies but represent technologies' interaction with the social, political and economic relations in which they appear, are developed and deployed. Rather than one or other of information society's dynamics being abnormal, both dynamics must be regarded as linked aspects of its character. However, the dominant distinction between normal (natural) and abnormal (transitory) tendencies renders whichever dynamic is favoured as the driving force behind the information society, while the other is regarded as a problem, a resistance or a misapprehension of the 'logic of informationalism'.

More importantly, both dynamics (taken alone) discourage political engagement: the determinism and fatalism of the enclosing dynamic is simplistic (and ideologically driven), asking us to accept developments as inevitable; the disclosing dynamic underestimates the resistance (both explicit and systemic) to the possibilities it highlights, and implicitly discourages action because democratic technics will 'naturally' triumph. Too often the history of ICTs is wrenched out of the history of technology and presented as something altogether separate and therefore different, rendering previous political, economic and social analyses irrelevant, and therefore no guide to political action. This is not the case: there are sufficient analytical tools to hand without the continual invention of new paradigms to understand the current stage of technological advance.

An account of the information society needs to accord to each dynamic an analytical importance which does not render the other as abnormal. This suggests that any analysis of the information society needs to recognize the challenges of enclosure to disclosure, and vice versa. These challenges are not temporary or transitory but are the way the global information society will develop (as previous technological ages have developed). Indeed, a political economy of the information society must recognize the implications of this dual dynamic as a complex system: not as contradictory and problematic. This allows us to retain the analyses of society as a complex of interacting interests that have been developed in the past. Thus the history of political and social thought that we have inherited in the new millennium is just as useful as it always was. There is no need to reinvent the wheel, or ignore previous conclusions about the character of the social relations of technology, if we want to understand the information age.

Sceptical yet Hopeful

Having spent much of this book maintaining a sceptical view about the impact of ICTs, I want to finish on a more positive note. This is not to say there are no difficult problems to overcome; however, the foregoing discussion does suggest (as it was meant to) that there are alternative trajectories, or different information societies that we can make real if we choose to. This will not be easy or inevitable, but in the same way that political (and economic) decisions have got us to where we are today, different decisions can move us in different directions. While clearly there are powerful social forces that have pushed the global information society (and its discourse) in this particular direction, there is no need to accept current developments as unavoidable or inevitable.

There is a closure evident in much of the discourse that surrounds the analysis of ICTs and their relation to society which is politically debilitating. Criticizing Manuel Castells's influential trilogy on the information age, Craig Calhoun argues that like much of the literature of the information society, there is 'a failure of imagination and a powerful presentation of current structures of the information age as inevitable' (2000: 47). The argument that 'there is no alternative' to the way ICTs have been deployed is a profoundly political argument, and only by realizing this can we then move to think about how the information society could develop differently. Ziauddin Sardar sums up the position well when he argues:

> in a very subtle way, predictions and forecasts silence debate and discussion. They present technology as an autonomous and desirable force and project the future as unavoidable. The desirable products of technology generate more desire; its undesirable side effects require more technology to solve them. We are locked in a linear, one-dimensional trajectory that has actually foreclosed the future. . . . There is no such thing as *the* future; there are many, many futures. And our concern should be with what the future ought to be, what we want it to be. (Sardar 1999: 27)

We need to question the assertions that are frequently made about the use, value and deployment of ICTs. By this I mean we need to be clear about why certain developments seem inevitable and why others are regarded as nonsensical, and we need to carefully examine such conclusions and challenge them if need be.

Already there is a growing notion of a global civil society alongside, or perhaps within, the global information society. This is evidenced in the growing movement to re-examine globalization, to question the multilateral governance of the global economy and to raise issues around human rights, as well as to further the historic advances made by women throughout the world in the last century.

Many of these political interventions have been enhanced by the use of ICTs. From issues around bio-piracy and intellectual property, to issues nearer home like surveillance and privacy over the internet, there is a slowly growing global constituency which is asking awkward questions about the role of ICTs in the future. However, these campaigns reside (currently) on the periphery of the political domain.

Part of the problem is that too often the (global) information society is perceived as something revolutionary and new to which older analyses have no relevance (even by those who want to work in some way against such developments). But if the information society is capitalistic then it makes sense to mobilize previous criticisms of capitalism to understand it. We can look to Marx, or Galbraith if you prefer, but as the recent experience of dotcom companies has revealed we cannot ignore the previously known 'rules' of economics. Indeed, the rising oil price at the turn of the millennium has led some to speculate that the 'new economy' which underpins the information society may have less to do with the deployment of ICTs, and a lot more to do with the historically low real price of oil in the 1990s (Oswald 2000). If this is so, a long period of high oil prices may bring the information society down to earth with a bump.

Similarly, we might have many different views of politics, from Isaiah Berlin's view of negative liberty, to views of social justice drawn from John Rawls, but politics is still about balancing interests and the use (and abuse) of authority, in the information society as before. Although the US Presidential election was hailed as the first of the information age, the American electorate in 2000 seemed largely to ignore the internet's capabilities in this regard, and were seldom interested in the candidates' coverage of 'new economy' issues (Fallows 2000). Elsewhere, the continuing debates (and disputes) about the shape of the European Union reveal that politics still involves many of the same actors (states, interest groups, political parties) that it always has in modern society. Politics seems to be remarkably unchanged by the information age (though, of course, we are still told that the *real* change is just round the corner). The emergence of the information society may change some of the forms in which our interactions take place, but the substance of our lives will remain the same: the need for sustenance, the need for companionship, the need to work to live.

We can recognize the possibilities and potentiality of the information society, but we have to make it happen, there is no 'natural' development path. If we want the global information society to be an improvement on contemporary global society then the responsibility lies with us; equally, where we do not want change in the way our societies handle certain issues (of which welfare is perhaps paramount), we should be wary of claims that the changes wrought by new technologies are inevitable. We need to be sceptical yet hopeful, we need to recognize the continuing interaction between the twin dynamics of the information society and not accept that any particular version of the information society (projected into the future) is inevitable, including our own preferred option. As before, (information) society will be what we make of it, and therefore the battle to conceive of the future is important and should not be left to the technicists, or the policy-makers alone. There is nothing natural, nothing inevitable about the information society: while we can only make our own history in the circumstances we find ourselves in, we should recognize that these circumstances are not as fixed or narrow as many commentators on the information society tell us.

Appendix
Intellectual Property

This appendix introduces the key aspects of intellectual property and an outline of the ways property in knowledge is often justified. A much fuller treatment of the subject is presented in my previous book (May 2000a), which develops an extended immanent critique of the three justificatory schemata I briefly outline in the second section.

What is intellectual property?

When knowledge becomes subject to ownership, intellectual property rights (IPRs) express ownership's legal benefits – most importantly, the ability to charge rent for use; to receive compensation for loss; and to receive payment for transfer. Intellectual property rights are subdivided into a number of groups, of which two generate most discussion: industrial intellectual property (patents), and literary or artistic intellectual property (copyrights). Conventionally the difference between patents and copyrights is presented as between a patent's protection of an idea, and copyright's protection of the expression of an idea. The balance between private reward and public interest has been traditionally expressed through time limits on IPRs, which is to say that, unlike material property, IPRs are formally temporary. Once their time has expired they are returned to the public realm of freely available knowledge.

For patents the knowledge which is to be registered and thus made property should be applicable in industry. To be patentable an idea must be:

- *new*, not already in the public domain or the subject of a previous patent;
- *non obvious*, so that it should not be commonsense to any accomplished practitioner in the field who, having been asked to solve a particular practical problem, would see this solution immediately, and it should not be self-evident using available skills or technologies;
- *useful*, or *applicable in industry*, so that it must have a stated function, and could immediately be produced to fulfil this function.

Following the harmonization of national legislation in the Trade Related Aspects of Intellectual Property Rights (TRIPs) agreement, if these three conditions are fulfilled then an idea can be patented in nearly every country of the world. The patent is lodged at the national patent office (or with the European Patent Office), which for an agreed fee will allow others access to the patented knowledge as expressed in the patent document, but perhaps more importantly the office will police and punish unauthorized usage. Patents are an institutionalized bargain between the state and the inventor. The state agrees to ensure the inventor is paid for their idea when others use it (for the term of the patent), and the inventor allows the state to lodge the idea in its public records.

Unlike patent, copyright is concerned with the form of knowledge and information that would normally be termed 'literary and artistic works'. This is usually expressed in words, symbols, music, pictures, three-dimensional objects, or some combination of these different forms. Copyright therefore covers literary works (fiction and non-fiction); musical works (of all sorts); artistic works (of two *and* three dimensional form and importantly irrespective of content – from 'pure art' and advertising to amateur drawings and your child's doodles); maps; technical drawings; photography; audiovisual works (including cinematic works, video and forms of multimedia); and audio recordings. In some jurisdictions this may stretch to broadcasts and also typographical arrangements of publications. However, the underlying ideas, the plot, the conjunction of colours does not receive protection – only the specific expression attracts copyright.

Copyright is meant to ensure that what is protected should not be reproduced without the express permission of the creator (or the owner of the copyright, which may have been legally transferred to another party by the creator). This is often limited to an economic right, where the creator (or copyright owner) is legally entitled to a share of any return that is earned by the utilization or reproduction of the copyrighted knowledge. In some jurisdictions, however (principally in continental Europe), there is an additional moral right not to have work tampered with or misrepresented. In all cases, failure to agree terms prior to the act of reproduction or duplication may result in any income being awarded to the original copyright holder by the court if an infringement is deemed to have taken place. Unlike patents, however, copyright resides in the work from the moment of creation; all that is required is that the creator can prove that any supposed infringement is a reproduction of the original work, in terms of content, and that it was the product of an intended action of copying.

Trademarks serve to distinguish the products of one company from another and can be made up of one or more distinctive words, letters, numbers, drawings or pictures, emblems or other graphic representations. Generally trademarks need to be registered, and in the act of registration a check is carried out to ensure that there are no other companies currently registering the same word, symbol or other representation as a trademark in the sector of the economy nominated by the registering company. A history of use of a trademark may establish its viability and support its subsequent legal recognition. Thus a particular trademark is unlikely to succeed in being registered if it is too similar to, or liable to cause confusion with, a trademark already registered by another company (referred to as 'passing off'). Neither will it attract protection if the term or symbol is already in common use. In some jurisdictions the outward manifestation of packaging, provided that it is not a form necessarily dictated by function, may also be subject to trademark status (of which the most famous case is the Coca-Cola bottle).

There are other sorts of intellectual property, from process patents (which are like patents but cover processes as opposed to actual machines) to geographical indicators (such as 'champagne'), but these share the key characteristics noted above: they code a form of information or knowledge as ownable property. It is sometimes also useful to think of trade secrets as intellectual property. Although a form which is not made public, trade secrets allow the control or ownership of knowledge. In one way the trade secret is the ultimate private knowledge property. However, while in some celebrated cases a trade secret is relied on to maintain a competitive advantage (and again the example of Coke is apposite, along with Kentucky Fried Chicken's 'secret blend of herbs and spices'), in the main those who rely on knowledge as a resource adopt an intellectual property approach to protection, rather than keeping such knowledge completely secret. Indeed, for the knowledge industries it would be counterproductive, impossible even, to function on the basis of knowledge being secret, given the importance of reproduction and transfer of that knowledge to generate income and profit. Intellectual property constructs a balance between public availability and private benefit which allows wider access to knowledge and information than trade secrecy. But this availability is only within specific legal limits constructed by intellectual property.

How is property in knowledge usually justified?

In the contemporary debates about information society, the assertion that there is a clear metaphorical link, indeed a workable similarity, between property in material objects and property in knowledge, information or intellectual creations is maintained as unproblematic. Here I will summarize the three justifications of intellectual property based on this metaphorical relationship, which I have explored at greater length elsewhere. Conventionally there are two philosophical schemes for justifying property and one more pragmatic justification, all of which are used to legitimize and support intellectual property in varying combinations, both in the academic literature and more popularly throughout the media. These arguments are to be heard in one form or another whenever IPRs are discussed.

The first position argues for labour's desert: the effort that is put into the improvement of nature requires that such effort should be rewarded. In John Locke's original formulation (for property) of 1690 this was modelled on the improvement of land. Thus the application of effort to produce crops and/or improved resource yields justified the ownership of specific tracts of land by the person who worked to produce such improvement. However, starting from this initial position, Locke moved on to argue that there was therefore also a right in disposal (or alienation), mediated by money. This led him to conclude that all property, even after its separation from the original labourer, could be justified on the basis that it had originally been produced through the labour of an individual. Thus property was justified as it was the just return for the efforts of those who produced it, and perhaps more importantly encouraged the improvement of nature through the reward of effort by producing a transferable resource (Locke 1988).

The Lockean argument thus supports property by suggesting that it is only through reward (the incidence of property) that human beings make any effort to improve the world. Property therefore plays an instrumental role in society by encouraging individual effort through the reward of ownership. In contemporary debates around intellectual property, this position, that patents, copyrights and other intellectual properties reward the effort that has been put into their development (the research investment made to develop a patented innovation, the marketing expense in establishing a trademark), is a commonplace regarding the justification of IPRs and appears in one form or another in almost all discussions of the politics of knowledge ownership.

However, especially in the realm of copyrights and trademarks, this labour desert argument is sometimes supported through the mobilization of a secondary justificatory schema: the notion of property's links with the self as proposed by Hegel (see for instance, Hegel 1967). In this position, the control and ownership of property is a significant part of the protection of individual autonomy and selfhood. It is the manner in which individuals protect themselves from the invasions and attacks of others. For Hegel, property, and the rights that are accorded to its owner, protect the individual from the state and competing individuals in society by allowing them to carve out a sovereign space for the self. Property rights are part of the maintenance and development of the individual's autonomy and are therefore justified on the basis of this result. Property is held against the state, which legislates its protection (and rights) as part of the bargain with civil society. Individuals allow the state to operate in certain areas but protect their individuality (and sovereignty) through the limitations that property rights put upon the state *vis-à-vis* the individual's own life and possessions.

In intellectual property law on the European continent, this philosophical approach supports the inalienable moral rights that creators retain over their copyrights even after their formal transfer to new owners. In Anglo-Saxon law this mode of justification has been less well received due to its implications for the issue of the final alienability (transferability) of property. Nonetheless, especially where 'passing off' of trademarks, and the use of copyrighted material are concerned (sampling of music and the 'abuse' of MP3 files, for instance), this justificatory schema can sometimes be noted in the calls for redress based on the diminution of reputation, or the ownership of (self) expression.

The third area of justification I call the pragmatic or economic argument for the commodification of property. While both of the justificatory schemata outlined above are often present in arguments for the protection of intellectual property, this additional and important justification concerns the efficient use of resources. There is a particular story of the emergence of property rights that argues that its emergence was a response to the needs of individuals wishing to allocate resources among themselves (May 2000a: 18–21). Without robust property rights actionable through the legal sanction of the state, trade at a distance could never have grown up and therefore the international system of trade (along with the division of labour) would have foundered. This story suggests that the justification of (intellectual) property rights is grounded in the fact that they arose to fulfil a particular function, the construction of markets for goods at a distance and with strangers. This allows for an increase in efficiency because as the division of labour spread out over the distance at which property rights were enforced, so more and more specialized labour (and technology) could be utilized. Here intellectual property rights are justified on the basis that they underpin a market structure that ensures the efficient use of valuable (or owned) knowledge resources.

These three justificatory schemata are by no means uncontested but they are widely appealed to and as such have some salience as argumentative narratives or tropes.

References

Academic sources

Adams, J. (1998) *The Next World War: Computers are the Weapons and the Front Line is Everywhere.* London: Hutchinson/Arrow.

Angell, I. (2000) *The New Barbarian Manifesto: How to Survive the Information Age.* London: Kogan Page.

Ansah, P. A. V. (1986) 'The Struggle for Rights and Values in Communications', in M. Trabner (ed.), *The Myth of the Information Revolution: Social and Ethical Implications of Communication Technology.* London: Sage.

Archer, M. (1990) 'Theory, Culture and Post-Industrial Society', in M. Featherstone (ed.), *Global Culture: Nationalism, Globalisation and Modernity.* London: Sage.

Aronowitz, S. and DiFazio, W. (1996) 'High Technology and Work Tomorrow', *Annals of the American Academy of Politics and Social Sciences*, no. 544 (March): 52–67.

Arquilla, J. and Ronfeldt, D. (eds) (1997) *In Athena's Camp: Preparing for Conflict in the Information Age.* Santa Monica: RAND.

Arrow, K. (1996) 'The Economics of Information: An Exposition', *Empirica* 23, 2: 119–28.

Avenell, S. and Thompson, H. (1994) 'Commodity Relations and the Forces of Production: The Theft and Defence of Intellectual Property', *Journal of Interdisciplinary Economics* 5, 1: 23–35.

Bain, P. and Taylor, P. (2000) 'Entrapped by the "Electronic Panoptican"? Worker Resistance in the Call Centre', *New Technology, Work and Employment* 15, 1 (March): 2–18.

Barbrook, R. (2000) 'Cyber-Communism: How the Americans are Superseding Capitalism in Cyberspace', *Science as Culture* 9, 1: 5–40.

Barbrook, R. and Cameron, A. (1996) 'The Californian Ideology', *Science as Culture* 26: 44–72.

Barlow, J. P. (1996) 'Selling Wines without Bottles', in P. Ludlow (ed.), *High Noon on the Electronic Frontier*. Cambridge, Mass.: MIT Press. (Also widely available on the internet, at numerous sites.)

Bell, D. (1974) *The Coming of Post-Industrial Society*. London: Heinemann Educational.

Belt, V., Richardson, R. and Webster, J. (2000) 'Women's Work in the Information Economy: The Case of Telephone Call Centres', *Information Communication and Society* 3, 3: 366–85.

Beniger, J. R. (1986) *The Control Revolution: Technological and Economic Origins of the Information Society*. Cambridge, Mass.: Harvard University Press.

Berger, P. L. and Luckman, T. (1971) *The Social Construction of Reality: A Treatise on the Sociology of Knowledge*. Harmondsworth: Penguin Books.

Berger, S. and Dore, R. (eds) (1996) *National Diversity and Global Capitalism*. Ithaca: Cornell University Press.

Berlin, I. (1997) 'Two Concepts of Liberty' (1958), in H. Hardy and R. Hausheer (eds), *Isaiah Berlin: The Proper Study of Mankind*. London: Chatto and Windus.

Bettig, R. (1997) 'The Enclosure of Cyberspace', *Critical Studies in Mass Communication* 14 (June): 138–57.

Bimber, B. (1995) 'Three Faces of Technological Determinism', in M. R. Smith and L. Marx (eds), *Does Technology Drive History: The Dilemma of Technological Determinism*. Cambridge, Mass.: MIT Press.

Bimber, B. (1998) 'The Internet and Political Transformation: Populism, Community and Accelerated Pluralism', *Polity* 31, 1 (Fall): 133–60.

Blank, S. J. (1997) 'Preparing for the Next War: Reflections on the Revolution in Military Affairs', in J. Arquilla and D. Ronfeldt (eds), *In Athena's Camp: Preparing for Conflict in the Information Age*. Santa Monica: RAND.

Boyle, J. (1996) *Shamans, Software and Spleens: Law and the Construction of the Information Society*. Cambridge, Mass.: Harvard University Press.

Braudel, F. (1982) *The Wheels of Commerce*, vol. 2 of *Civilisation and Capitalism, 15th–18th Century*. London: William Collins.

Bronfenbrenner, K. (2000) *Uneasy Terrain: The Impact of Capital Mobility on Workers, Wages and Union Organizing*, testimony to the US Trade Deficit Review Commission. Ithaca: New York State School of Industrial and Labour Relations, Cornell University.

Brown, D. (1997) *Cybertrends: Chaos, Power and Accountability in the Information Age*. London: Viking.

Bruckman, A. S. (1996) 'Gender Swapping on the Internet', in P. Ludlow (ed.), *High Noon on the Electronic Frontier*. Cambridge, Mass.: MIT Press.

Cairncross, F. (1998) *The Death of Distance: How the Communications Revolution will Change our Lives*. London: Orion Business Books.

Calabrese, A. (1997) 'Creative Destruction? From the Welfare State to the Global Information Society', *Javnost – The Public* 4, 4: 7–24.

Calhoun, C. (1998) 'Community without Propinquity Revisited: Communications Technology and the Transformation of the Urban Public Sphere', *Sociological Inquiry* 68, 3 (August): 373–97.

Camus, A. (1969) *The Rebel* (1953). Harmondsworth: Penguin/Peregrine.

Castells, M. (1996) *The Rise of Network Society*, vol. 1 of *The Information Age: Economy, Society and Culture*. Oxford: Blackwell.

Castells, M. (1997a) *The Power of Identity*, vol. 2 of *The Information Age: Economy, Society and Culture*. Oxford: Blackwell.

Castells, M. (1997b) 'An Introduction to the Information Age', *City* 7 (May): 6–16.

Castells, M. (1998) *End of Millennium*, vol. 3 of *The Information Age: Economy, Society and Culture*. Oxford: Blackwell.

Castells, M. (2000) 'Information Technology and Global Capitalism', in W. Hutton and A. Giddens (eds), *On The Edge: Living with Global Capitalism*. London: Jonathan Cape.

Ceruzzi, P. (1997) 'An Unforeseen Revolution: Computers and Expectations 1935–1985' (1986), in A. H. Teich (ed.), *Technology and the Future*, 7th edn. New York: St Martin's Press.

Chadwick, A. (1999) *Augmenting Democracy*. Aldershot: Ashgate.

Chandler, A. D. and Cortada, J. W. (eds) (2000) *A Nation Transformed by Information*. New York: Oxford University Press.

Cleaver, H. (1998) 'The Zapatista Effect: The Internet and the Rise of an Alternative Political Fabric', *Journal Of International Affairs* (Technology and International Policy issue) 51, 2 (Spring): 621–40.

Cleveland, H. (1985) 'The Twilight of Hierarchy: Speculation on the Global Information Society', in B. R. Guile (ed.), *Information Technologies and Social Transformation*. Washington DC: National Academy Press.

Corrigan, P. and Sayer, D. (1981) 'How the Law Rules: Variations on Some Themes in Karl Marx', in B. Fryer, A. Hunt, D. McBarnet and B. Moorhouse (eds), *Law, State and Society*. London: Croom Helm.

Coyle, D. (1997) *The Weightless World: Strategies for Managing in the Digital Economy*. Oxford: Capstone.

Curtis, P. (1996) 'MUDing: Social Phenomena in Text-based Virtual Realities', in P. Ludlow (ed.), *High Noon on the Electronic Frontier*. Cambridge, Mass.: MIT Press.

Cutler, C., Haufler, V. and Porter, T. (eds) (1998) *Private Authority in International Affairs*. Albany: State University of New York Press.

Day, P. and Harris, K. (1997) *Down-to-Earth Vision: Community Based IT Initiatives and Social Inclusion*. London: IBM/Community Development Foundation.

de Sola Pool, I. (1998) 'Foresight and Hindsight: The Case of the Telephone' (1977), in L. S. Etheridge (ed.), *Politics in Wired Nations: Selected Writings of Ithiel de Sola Pool*. New Brunswick: Transaction.

Dehqanzada, Y. A. and Florini, A. M. (2000) *Secrets for Sale: How Commercial Satellite Imagery will Change the World.* Washington DC: Carnegie Endowment for International Peace.

Dertouzos, M. (1997) *What Will Be: How the New World of Information will Change our Lives.* London: Piatkus.

Dibbell, J. (1999) *My Tiny Life: Crime and Passion in a Virtual World.* London: Fourth Estate.

Dicken, P. (1997) 'Transnational Corporations and Nation-States', *International Social Science Journal* 151 (March): 77–89.

Dicken, P. (1998) *Global Shift: Transforming the World Economy*, 3rd edn. London: Paul Chapman.

Dizard, W. P. (1982) *The Coming Information Age: An Overview of Technology, Economics and Politics.* New York: Longman.

Dordick, H. S. and Wang, G. (1993) *The Information Society: A Retrospective View.* Newbury Park: Sage.

Drahos, P. (1996) 'Global Law Reform and Rent-Seeking: The Case of Intellectual Property', *Australian Journal of Corporate Law* 7: 45–61.

Drucker, P. (1968) *The Age of Discontinuity: Guidelines to our Changing Society.* New York: Harper and Row.

Drucker, P. (1993) *Post-Capitalist Society.* New York: HarperBusiness.

Drucker, P. (1997) 'The Global Economy and the Nation-State', *Foreign Affairs* 76, 5 (Sept./Oct.): 159–71.

Duff, A. S. (2000) *Information Society Studies.* London: Routledge.

Dutton, W. H. (1999) *Society on the Line: Information Politics in the Digital Age.* Oxford: Oxford University Press.

Dyson, E. (1997) *Release 2.0: A Design for Living in the Digital Age.* London: Viking.

Dyson, E., Gilder, G., Keyworth, J. and Toffler, A. (1994) 'A Magna Carta for the Knowledge Age', Release 1.2, available at www.pff.org/position_old.html (17 Feb. 2000).

Eisenstein, E. L. (1980) *The Printing Press as an Agent of Change*, combined paperback volume. Cambridge: Cambridge University Press.

Esping-Andersen, G. (1999) *Social Foundations of Post-industrial Economies.* Oxford: Oxford University Press.

Evans, P. (1997) 'The Eclipse of the State? Reflections on Stateness in an Era of Globalisation', *World Politics* 50 (Oct.): 62–87.

Everard, J. (2000) *Virtual States: The Internet and the Boundaries of the Nation-State.* London: Routledge.

Fernie, S. (1998) 'Hanging on the Telephone', *CentrePiece* 3, 1 (Spring): 6–11.

Ford, M. (1998) *Surveillance and Privacy at Work.* London: Institute of Employment Rights.

Frankel, B. (1987) *The Post-Industrial Utopians.* Cambridge: Polity.

Fraser, M. (1999) *Free-for-All: The Struggle for Dominance on the Digital Frontier.* Toronto: Stoddent.

Freedman, L. (1998) *The Revolution in Strategic Affairs*, Adelphi Paper 318. London: Oxford University Press/International Institute for Strategic Studies.

Freeman, C., Soete, L. and Efendioglu, U. (1995) 'Diffusion and the Employment Effects of Information and Communication Technology', *International Labour Review* 134, 4–5: 587–603.

Frenkel, S. J., Korczynski, M., Shire, K. A. and Tam, M. (1999) *On The Front Line: Organization of Work in the Information Economy*, Cornell International Industrial and Labour Relations Report 35. Ithaca: Cornell University Press.

Friedrichs, G. and Schaff, A. (eds) (1982) *Microelectronics and Society: For Better or for Worse*. Oxford: Pergamon Press.

Fuller, S. (1998) 'Why Even Scholars Don't Get a Free Lunch in Cyberspace', in B. Loader (ed.), *Cyberspace Divide: Equality, Agency and Policy in the Information Society*. London: Routledge.

Garratt, S. (1998) *Adventures in Wonderland: A Decade of Club Culture*. London: Headline.

Gates, B. (1996) *The Road Ahead*, 2nd edn. London: Penguin Books.

Gaur, A. (1992) *A History of Writing*, rev. edn. London: British Library.

Golding, P. (2000) 'Forthcoming Features: Information and Communications Technologies and the Sociology of the Future', *Sociology* 34, 1 (Feb.): 165–84.

Gouré, D. (1996) 'The Impact of the Information Revolution on Strategy and Doctrine', in S. J. D. Schwartzstein (ed.), *The Information Revolution and National Security: Dimensions and Directions*. Washington DC: Center for Strategic and International Studies.

Gray, C. S. (1996) 'A Rejoinder [to Martin Libicki]', *Orbis* 40, 2 (Spring): 274–6.

Gurak, L. J. (1999) 'The Promise and the Peril of Social Action in Cyberspace: *Ethos*, Delivery and the Protests over MarketPlace and the Clipper Chip', in P. Kollock and M. A. Smith (eds), *Communities in Cyberspace*. London: Routledge.

Hafner, K. and Lyon, M. (1996) *Where Wizards Stay Up Late: The Origins of the Internet*. New York: Simon and Schuster.

Halcli, A. and Webster, F. (2000) 'Inequality and Mobilisation in *The Information Age*', *European Journal of Social Theory* 3, 1 (Feb.): 67–81.

Hamelink, C. (1986) 'Is There Life after the Information Revolution?', in M. Trabner (ed.), *The Myth of the Information Revolution: Social and Ethical Implications of Communication Technology*. London: Sage.

Handy, C. (1994) *The Empty Raincoat: Making Sense of the Future*. London: Hutchinson.

Hanson, R. L. (1989) 'Democracy', in T. Ball, J. Farr and R. L. Hanson (eds), *Political Innovation and Conceptual Change*. Cambridge: Cambridge University Press.

Haywood, T. (1998) 'Global Networks and the Myth of Equality', in B. Loader (ed.), *Cyberspace Divide*. London: Routledge.

Heeks, R., Krishna, S., Nicholson, B. and Sahay, S. (2000) 'Synching or Sinking: Trajectories and Strategies in Global Software Outsourcing Relationships', Development Informatics, Working Paper 9, Institute for Development Policy and Management, University of Manchester, available at www.man.ac.uk/idpm/idpm_dp.htm#devinf_wp (25 Oct. 2000).

Hegel, G. (1967) *Philosophy of Right* (1821). Oxford: Oxford University Press.

Helleiner, E. (1999) 'State Power and the Regulation of Illicit Activity in Global Finance', in H. R. Friman and P. Andreas (eds), *The Illicit Global Economy and State Power*. Lanham: Rowman and Littlefield.

Hellman, J. A. (1999) 'Real and Virtual Chiapas: Magic Realism and the Left', in Leo Panitch and Colin Leys (eds), *Necessary and Unnecessary Utopias: Socialist Register 2000*. Rendlesham: Merlin Press.

Hill, K. A. and Hughes, J. E. (1998) *Cyberpolitics: Citizen Activism in the Age of the Internet*. Lanham: Rowman and Littlefield.

Hirst, P. and Thompson, G. (1999) *Globalization in Question*, 2nd edn. Cambridge: Polity.

Hobsbawm, E. (1994) *Age of Extremes: The Short Twentieth Century 1914–1991*. London: Michael Joseph.

Hochschild, A. R. (1983) *The Managed Heart: Commercialization of Human Feeling*. Berkeley: University of California Press.

Hodgson, G. M. (1999) *Economics and Utopia*. London: Routledge.

Huws, U. (1999) 'Material World: The Myth of the Weightless Economy', in L. Panitch and C. Leys (eds), *Global Capitalism versus Democracy* (Socialist Register 1999). Rendlesham: Merlin Press.

IBM (1997) *The Net Result: Social Inclusion in the Information Society*. London: IBM Corporate Affairs.

IER (Institute of Employment Rights) (2000) *Employment Rights: Building on Fairness at Work*. London: IER.

IPSO (Information Society Project Office) (1998) *Information Technologies, Productivity and Employment*, Report to DGIII – Industry. Brussels: IPSO, available at www.ipso.cec.be/infosoc/promo/pubs/prodep.html (14 Jan. 1998).

Jayasuriya, K. (1999) 'Globalisation, Law and the Transformation of Sovereignty: The Emergence of Global Regulatory Governance', *Global Legal Studies Journal* 6: 425–55.

Johns, A. (1998) *The Nature of the Book: Print and Knowledge in the Making*. Chicago: Chicago University Press.

Jones, R. J. B. (2000) *The World Turned Upside Down? Globalisation and the Future of the State*. Manchester: Manchester University Press.

Kaldor, M. (1999) *New and Old Wars: Organised Violence in a Global Era*. Cambridge: Polity.

Kay, J. (1993) *Foundations of Corporate Success: How Business Strategies Add Value*. Oxford: Oxford University Press.

Keohane, R. O. and Nye, J. S. (1998) 'Power and Interdependence in the Information Age', *Foreign Affairs* 77, 5 (Sept.–Oct): 81–94.

Klein, N. (2001) *No Logo*. London: Flamingo.

Kollock, P. (1999) 'The Economies of On-line Co-operation: Gifts and Public Goods in Cyberspace', in P. Kollock and M. A. Smith (eds), *Communities in Cyberspace*. London: Routledge.

Kollock, P. and Smith, M. A. (eds) (1999) *Communities in Cyberspace*. London: Routledge.

Kotkin, J. (2000) *The New Geography: How the Digital Revolution is Reshaping the American Landscape*. New York: Random House.

Kraut, R., Patterson, M., Lundmark, V., Kiesler, S., Mukopadhyay, T. and Scherlis, W. (1998) 'Internet Paradox: A Social Technology that Reduces Social Involvement and Psychological Well-Being?', *American Psychologist* 53, 9 (Sept.): 1017–31.

Kumar, K. (1978) *Prophecy and Progress: The Sociology of Industrial and Post-Industrial Society*. Harmondsworth: Penguin Books.

Kumar, K. (1995) *From Post-industrial to Post-modern Society: New Theories of the Contemporary World*. Oxford: Blackwell.

Lash, S. and Urry, J. (1994) *Economies of Signs and Space*. London: Sage.

Leadbeater, C. (1999) *Living on Thin Air: The New Economy*. London: Viking.

Lefebvre, H. (1991) *The Production of Space*. Oxford: Blackwell.

Lessig, L. (1999) *Code and Other Laws of Cyberspace*. New York: Basic Books.

Levinson, P. (1997) *The Soft Edge: A Natural History and Future of the Information Revolution*. London: Routledge.

Libicki, M. C. (1998) 'Information War, Information Peace', *Journal of International Affairs* (Technology and International Policy issue) 51, 2 (Spring): 411–28.

Litman, J. (1991) 'Copyright as Myth', *University of Pittsburgh Law Review* 53: 235–49.

Loader, B. (1998) 'Cyberspace Divide: Equality, Agency and Policy in the Information Society', in B. Loader (ed.), *Cyberspace Divide*. London: Routledge.

Locke, J. (1988) *Two Treatises on Government*. (1690). Cambridge: Cambridge University Press.

Lukes, S. (1974) *Power: A Radical View*. Basingstoke: Macmillan Education.

Lyon, D. (1988) *The Information Society: Issues and Illusions*. Cambridge: Polity.

Lyon, D. (2001) *Surveillance Society: Monitoring everyday life*. Buckingham: Open University Press.

MacBride, S. et al. (1980) *Many Voices One World: Communication and Society, Today and Tomorrow*. London: Kogan Page/UNESCO.

McLuhan, M. (1962) *The Gutenberg Galaxy*. Toronto: University of Toronto Press.

McLuhan, M. (1994) *Understanding Media: The Extensions of Man* (1965). Cambridge, Mass.: MIT Press.

Mansell, R. and Wehn, U. (1998) *Knowledge Societies: Information Technology for Sustainable Development*. Oxford: United Nations Commission on Science and Technology for Development/Oxford University Press.

Margetts, H. (1999) *Information Technology in Government: Britain and America*. London: Routledge.

Marglin, S. A. (1974) 'What Do Bosses Do? The Origins and Functions of Hierarchy in Capitalist Production', *Review of Radical Political Economics* 6, 2 (Summer): 33–60.

Martin, W. J. (1995) *The Global Information Society*. Aldershot: Aslib/Gower.

Marvin, C. (1987) 'Information and History', in J. D. Slack and F. Fejes (eds), *The Ideology of the Information Age*. Norwood, NJ.: Ablex.

Marx, K. (1974a) *Capital: A Critical Analysis of Capitalist Production*, vol. 1 (1887). London: Lawrence and Wishart.

Marx, K. (1974b) *Capital: A Critique of Political Economy*, vol. 3. London: Lawrence and Wishart.

Marx, K. and Engels, F. (1967) *The Communist Manifesto* (1888). Harmondsworth: Penguin.

Massey, D. (1985) 'Which "New Technology"?', in M. Castells (ed.), *High Technology, Space and Society* (Urban Affairs Annual Review 28). Beverly Hills: Sage.

Masuda, Y. (1990) *Managing in the Information Society: Releasing Synergy Japanese Style*, foreword by Ronnie Lessem. Oxford: Blackwell. First published as Y. Masuda, *The Information Society as Post-industrial Society*, Tokyo: Institute for Information Society, 1980.

Mathews, J. T. (1997) 'Power Shift', *Foreign Affairs* 76, 1 (Jan.–Feb.): 50–66.

May, C. (2000a) *A Global Political Economy of Intellectual Property Rights: The New Enclosures?*, RIPE series. London: Routledge.

May, C. (2000b) 'Information Society, Task Mobility and the End of Work', *Futures* 32, 5 (May): 399–416.

May, C. (2000c) 'The Information Society as Mega-Machine: The Continuing Relevance of Lewis Mumford', *Information Communication and Society* 3, 2 (Summer): 241–65.

Metzl, J. F. (1996) 'Information Technology and Human Rights', *Human Rights Quarterly* 18 (Nov.): 705–46.

Mills, C. W. (1953) *White Collar: The American Middle Classes*. New York: Oxford University Press.

Mitchell, W. J. (1995) *City of Bits: Space, Place and the Infobahn*. Cambridge, Mass.: MIT Press.

Moore, N. (1997) 'Neo-Liberal or Dirigiste? Policies for an Information Society' *Political Quarterly* 8, 3 (July–Sept.): 276–83.

Morris-Suzuki, T. (1988) *Beyond Computopia: Information, Automation and Democracy in Japan*. London: Kegan Paul International.

Mumford, L. (1962) 'Apology to Henry Adams', *Virginia Quarterly Review* 38 (Spring): 196–217.

Mumford, L. (1964) 'Authoritarian and Democratic Technics', *Technology and Culture* 5 (Winter): 1–8.

Mumford, L. (1966a) 'Technics and the Nature of Man', *Technology and Culture* 7: 303–17.

Mumford, L. (1966b) *Technics and Human Development*, vol. 1 of *Myth of the Machine*. New York: Harcourt Brace Jovanovich.

Mumford, L. (1971) *The Pentagon of Power*, vol. 2 of *Myth of the Machine*. London: Secker and Warburg.

Naisbitt, J. (1984) *Megatrends: Ten New Directions Transforming our Lives*. London: Macdonald/Futura.

NAO (National Audit Office) (1999) *Government on the Web*. London: Stationery Office.

Negroponte, N. (1995) *Being Digital*. London: Coronet/Hodder and Stoughton.

Netanel, N. W. (2000) 'Cyberspace Self-Governance: A Sceptical View from Liberal Democratic Theory', *California Law Review* 88, 2 (March): 395–498.

Noble, D. F. (1979) *America by Design: Science, Technology and the Rise of Corporate Capitalism*. Oxford: Oxford University Press.

Nora, S. and Minc, A. (1980) *The Computerization of Society*. Cambridge, Mass.: MIT Press.

Noveck, B. S. (2000) 'Paradoxical Partners: Electronic Communication and Electronic Democracy', *Democratization* 7, 1: 18–35.

O'Brien, R. (1992) *Global Financial Integration: The End of Geography*. London: Royal Institute of International Affairs/Pinter.

Ohmae, K. (1990) *The Borderless World: Power and Strategy in the Inter-linked Economy*. London: Collins.

OECD (Organisation for Economic Co-operation and Development) (1997) *Towards a Global Information Society*. Paris: OECD.

OECD (Organisation for Economic Co-operation and Development) (1998) *Impact of the Emerging Information Society on the Policy Development Process and Democratic Quality*. Paris: OECD.

Palan, R. (1998) 'Trying to Have Your Cake and Eating It: How and Why the State System has Created Offshore', *International Studies Quarterly* 42 (Dec.): 625–44.

Palan, R. and Abbot, J. (1996) *State Strategies in the Global Political Economy*. London: Pinter.

Panitch, L. (1996) 'Rethinking the Role of the State', in J. H. Mittelman (ed.), *Globalisation: Critical Reflections* (IPE Yearbook 9). Boulder: Lynne Rienner.

Penrose, E. (1995) *The Theory of the Growth of the Firm* (1959), 3rd edn with a new foreword. Oxford: Oxford University Press.

Perelman, M. (1998) *Class Warfare in the Information Age*. New York: St Martin's Press.

Poirier, R. (1990) 'The Information Economy Approach: Characteristics, Limitations and Future Prospects', *The Information Society* 7, 4: 245–85.

Porat, M. U. (1978) 'Global Implication of the Information Society', *Journal of Communication* 28, 1 (Winter): 70–80.

Posner, R. A. (1998) 'Creating a Legal Framework for Economic Development', *World Bank Research Observer* 13, 1 (Feb.): 1–11.

Post, D. (1996) 'Jefferson Ascendant', available at www.cli.org/DPost/X0011_JEFFHAM.html (26 July 2000).

Poster, M. (1990) *The Mode of Information: Poststructuralism and Social Context.* Cambridge: Polity.

Prasad, M. (1998) 'International Capital on "Silicon Plateau": Work and Control in India's Computer Industry', *Social Forces* 77, 2 (Dec.): 429–52.

Prügl, E. (1996) 'Home-Based Producers in Development Discourse', in E. Boris and E. Prügl (eds), *Homeworkers in Global Perspective: Invisible No More.* London: Routledge.

Raab, C. (1995) 'Connecting Orwell to Athens? Information Superhighways and the Privacy Debate', in W. B. H. J. van de Donk, I. Th. M. Snellen and P. W. Tops (eds), *Orwell in Athens: A Perspective on Informationalisation and Democracy.* Amsterdam: IOS Press.

Raab, C., Bellamy, C., Taylor, J., Dutton, W. H. and Peltu, M. (1996) 'The Information Polity: Electronic Democracy, Privacy, and Surveillance', in W. H. Dutton (ed.), *Information and Communication Technologies: Visions and Realities.* Oxford: Oxford University Press.

Raymond, E. (1998) 'The Cathedral and the Bazaar', available at sagan/earthspace.net/~esr/cathedral-bazaar/cathedral-bazaar.sgml(19Nov.1998), and at other sites.

Reich, R. (1991) *The Work of Nations: Preparing Ourselves for 21st-Century Capitalism.* London: Simon and Schuster.

Reid, E. (1998) 'The Self and the Internet: Variations on the Illusion of One Self', in J. Gackenbach (ed.), *Psychology and the Internet: Intrapersonal, Interpersonal and Transpersonal Implications.* San Diego: Academic Press.

Rheingold, H. (1996) 'A Slice of my Life in my Virtual Community', in P. Ludlow (ed.), *High Noon on the Electronic Frontier.* Cambridge, Mass.: MIT Press.

Richardson, R. (1994) 'Back-Officing Front Office Functions – Organisational and Locational Implications of New Telemediated Services', in R. Mansell (ed.), *The Management of Information and Communication Technologies: Emerging Patterns of Control.* London: Aslib.

Rifkin, J. (1996) *The End of Work: The Decline of the Global Labour Force and the Dawn of the Post-Market Era.* New York: Putnam.

Rifkin, J. (1998) *The Biotech Century: The Coming Age of Genetic Commerce.* London: Victor Gollancz.

Robins, K. and Webster, F. (1999) *Times of the Technoculture: From the Information Society to the Virtual Life.* London: Routledge.

Rosenberg, N. (1982) 'Marx as a student of technology' (1976), in *Inside the Black Box: Technology and Economics.* Cambridge: Cambridge University Press.

Rueschemeyer, D. (1986) *Power and the Division of Labour.* Stanford: Stanford University Press.

Rueschemeyer, D. and Putterman, L. (1992) 'Synergy or Rivalry?', in L. Putterman and D. Rueschemeyer (eds), *State and Market in Development: Synergy or rivalry?* Boulder: Lynne Rienner.

Rushkoff, D. (1994) *Cyberia: Life in the Trenches of Hyperspace.* London: Flamingo/HarperCollins.

Sayer, A. and Walker, R. (1992) *The New Social Economy: Reworking the Division of Labour.* Oxford: Blackwell.

Schaff, A. (1982) 'Occupations versus Work', in G. Friedrichs and A. Schaff (eds), *Microelectronics and Society: For Better or for Worse.* Oxford: Pergamon Press.

Schalken, K. (2000) 'Virtual Communities: New Public Sphere on the Internet?', in J. Hoff, I. Horrocks and P. Tops (eds), *Democratic Governance and New Technology: Technologically mediated innovations in political practice in Western Europe.* London: Routledge.

Schmitz, J. (1997) 'Structural Relations, Electronic Media and Social Change: The Public Electronic Network and the Homeless', in S. G. Jones (ed.), *Virtual Culture: Identity and Communication in Cybersociety.* London: Sage.

Schnaars, S. P. (1989) *Megamistakes: Forecasting and the Myth of Rapid Technological Change.* New York: Free Press.

Schwartz, P. M. (1999) 'Privacy and Democracy in Cyberspace', *Vanderbilt Law Review* 52, 6 (Nov.): 1609–702.

Schwartzstein, S. J. D. (ed.) (1996) *The Information Revolution and National Security: Dimensions and Directions.* Washington DC: Center for Strategic and International Studies.

Scott, A. and Street, J. (2000) 'From Media Politics to E-Protest: The Use of Popular Culture and New Media in Parties and Social Movements', *Information Communication and Society* 3, 2: 215–40.

Sell, S. K. (1998) *Power and Ideas: North–South Politics of Intellectual Property and Antitrust.* Albany, N.Y.: State University of New York Press.

Sell, S. K. and May, C. (2001) 'Moments in Law: Contestation and Settlement in the History of Intellectual Property', *Review of International Political Economy* 8, 3 (Autumn): 467–500.

Servaes, J. and Burgelman, J.-C. (2000) 'In Search of a European Model for the Information Society. Editorial', *Telematics and Informatics* 17: 1–7.

Shulman, S. (1999) *Owning the Future.* Boston: Houghton Mifflin.

Sica, V. (2000) 'Cleaning the Laundry: States and the Monitoring of the Financial System', *Millennium: Journal of International Studies* 29, 1: 47–72.

Slack, J. D. (1984) 'The Information Revolution as Ideology', *Media Culture and Society* 6: 247–56.

Smith, A. (1996) *Software for the Self: Technology and Culture.* London: Faber and Faber.

Smith, C. and Thompson, P. (1998) 'Re-evaluating the Labour Process Debate', *Economic and Industrial Democracy* 19: 551–77.

Smith, D. A., Solinger, D. J. and Topik, S. C. (eds) (1999) *States and Sovereignty in the Global Economy*. London: Routledge.

Smith, M. A. (1999) 'Invisible Crowds in Cyberspace: Mapping the Social Structure of the Usenet', in P. Kollock and M. A. Smith (eds), *Communities in Cyberspace*. London: Routledge.

Smith, T. (2000) *Technology and Capital in the Age of Lean Production: A Marxian Critique of the 'New Economy'*. Albany: State University of New York Press.

Spencer, G. (1996) 'Microcybernetics as the Meta-Technology of Pure Control', in Z. Sardar and J. R. Ravetz (eds), *Cyberfutures: Culture and Politics on the Information Superhighway*. London: Pluto Press.

Standage, T. (1998) *The Victorian Internet*. London: Weidenfeld and Nicolson.

Stanworth, C. (1998) 'Telework and the Information Age', *New Technology, Work and Employment* 13, 1 (Mar.): 51–62.

Steffik, M. (1999) *The Internet Edge: Social, Legal and Technological Challenges for a Networked World*. Cambridge, Mass: MIT Press.

Steward, B. (2000) 'Teleworking: Good for Whose Health', in *Virtual Society? Get Real* (4–5 May) (paper abstracts). Uxbridge: Virtual Society? Programme/Brunel University.

Stoll, C. (1995) *Silicon Snake Oil: Second Thoughts on the Information Highway*. New York: Doubleday.

Stonier, T. (1983) *The Wealth of Information: A Profile of the Post-Industrial Economy*. London: Methuen.

Strange, S. (1996) *The Decline of the State: Power in the World Economy*. Cambridge: Cambridge University Press.

Strange, S. (1998) 'Globaloney?', *Review of International Political Economy* 5, 4 (Winter): 704–20.

Stremlau, J. (1996) 'Dateline Bangalore: Third World Technopolis', *Foreign Policy* 102 (Spring): 152–68.

Tapscott, D. (1996) *The Digital Economy: Promise and Peril in the Age of Networked Intelligence*. New York: McGraw-Hill.

Tapscott, D. (1998) *Growing Up Digital: The Rise of the Net Generation*. New York: McGraw-Hill.

Taylor, J., Bellamy, C., Raab, C., Dutton, W. H. and Peltu, M. (1996) 'Innovation in Public Service Delivery', in W. H. Dutton (ed.), *Information and Communication Technologies: Visions and Realities*. Oxford: Oxford University Press.

Taylor, S. (1998) 'Emotional Labour and the New Workplace', in P. Thompson and C. Warhurst (eds), *Workplaces of the Future*. Basingstoke: Macmillan Business.

Thomas, D. (1969) *A Long Time Burning: The History of Literary Censorship in England*. New York: Frederick A. Praeger.

Thompson, B. (2000) *New Mutualism: e-Mutualism or the Tragedy of the Dot.commons*. London: Co-operative Party.

Thompson, E. P. (1980) *The Making of the English Working Class* (1963). London: Penguin Books.

Thurow, L. C. (2000) 'Globalization: The Product of a Knowledge-Based Economy', *Annals of the American Academy* 570 (July): 19–31.

Toffler, A. (1970) *Future Shock*. London: Pan Books.

Toffler, A. (1980) *The Third Wave*. London: Collins.

Toffler, A. and Toffler, H. (1993) *War and Anti-War: Survival at the Dawn of the 21st Century*. Boston: Little Brown.

Tops, P., Horrocks, I. and Hoff, J. (2000) 'New Technology and Democratic Renewal', in J. Hoff, I. Horrocks and P. Tops (eds), *Democratic Governance and New Technology: Technologically Mediated Innovations in Political Practice in Western Europe*. London: Routledge.

Trachtman, J. P. (1998) 'Cyberspace, Sovereignty, Jurisdiction and Modernism', *Indiana Journal of Global Legal Studies* 5, 2: 561–81.

TUC (Trades Union Congress) (1998) *Job and Go!* London: TUC.

Turkle, S. (1997) *Life on the Screen: Identity in the Age of the Internet*. London: Phoenix.

Van Dijk, J. (1999) *The Network Society: Social Aspects of New Media*. London: Sage.

Vogel, S. K. (1996) *Freer Markets, More Rules: Regulatory Reform in Advanced Industrial Countries*. Ithaca: Cornell University Press.

Wade, R. (1996) 'Globalization and its Limits: Reports of the Death of the National Economy are Greatly Exaggerated', in S. Berger and R. Dore (eds), *National Diversity and Global Capitalism*. Ithaca: Cornell University Press.

Walker, R. A. (1999) 'Putting Capital in its Place: Globalisation and the Prospects for Labour', *Geoforum* 30, 3: 263–84.

Warhurst, C. and Thompson, P. (1998) 'Hands, Hearts and Minds: Changing Work and Workers at the End of the Century', in P. Thompson and C. Warhurst (eds), *Workplaces of the Future*. Basingstoke: Macmillan Business.

Webster, F. (1995) *Theories of the Information Society*. London: Routledge.

Webster, F. and Robins, K. (1989) 'Plan and Control: Towards a Cultural History of the Information Society', *Theory and Society* 18, 3 (May): 323–51.

Weiss, L. (1998) *The Myth of the Powerless State: Governing the Economy in a Global Era*. Cambridge: Polity.

Weiss, L. (1999) 'Globalisation and National Governance: Antimony or Interdependence', *Review of International Studies* 25 (special issue) (Dec.): 59–88.

White Paper (1999) *Modernising Government*. London: Stationery Office, available at www.citu.gov.uk/moderngov/whitepaper/4310.htm (21 Jan. 2000).

Williams, R. (1974) *Television: Technology and Cultural Form*. London: Fontana.

Williams, R. (1976) *Keywords: A Vocabulary of Culture and Society*. New York: Oxford University Press.

Wilson, M. I. (1998) 'Information Networks: The Global Offshore Labour Force', in G. Sussman and J. A. Lent (eds), *Global Productions: Labour in the Making of the 'Information Society'*. Cresskill, N.J.: Hampton Press.

Winner, L. (1978) *Autonomous Technology: Technics-Out-of-Control as a Theme in Political Thought*. Cambridge, Mass.: MIT Press.

Winner, L. (1995) 'Citizen Virtues in a Technological Order' (1992), in A. Feenberg and A. Hannay (eds), *Technology and the Politics of Knowledge*. Bloomington: Indiana University Press.

Winston, B. (1998) *Media Technology and Society: A History: From the Telegraph to the Internet*. London: Routledge.

Wolman, W. and Colamosca, A. (1997) *The Judas Economy: The Triumph of Capital and the Betrayal of Work*. Reading, Mass.: Addison-Wesley.

Wood, E. M. (1997) 'Modernity, Postmodernity or Capitalism?', *Review of International Political Economy* 4, 3 (Autumn): 539–60.

World Bank (1997) *World Development Report 1997: The State in a Changing World*. New York: Oxford University Press.

World Bank (1999) *World Development Report 1998/99: Knowledge for Development*. New York: Oxford University Press.

Wriston, W. B. (1997) 'Bits, Bytes and Diplomacy', *Foreign Affairs* 76, 5 (Sept.–Oct.): 172–82.

Zelwietro, J. (1998) 'The Politicisation of Environmental Organisations through the Internet', *Information Society* 14, 1 (Jan.–Mar.): 45–56.

Zuboff, S. (1988) *In The Age of the Smart Machine: The Future of Work and Power*. Oxford: Heinemann Professional.

News media sources

Anson, R. S. (1998) 'Apocalypse 2000? Millennium Crisis: A Ticking Time Bomb', *Observer*, 13 Dec., p. 15.

Arlidge, J. (2001) 'Beware – You've Got mail', *Observer*, 7 Jan., p. 18.

Borger, J. (2000a) 'US Mounts $2bn Offensive against Cyber-Terrorists', *Guardian*, 8 Jan., p. 2.

Borger, J. (2000b) 'Workers' Rights Abused in US', *Guardian*, 30 Aug., p. 12.

Brown, J. M. (2000) 'Jumping on Bandwidth for Internet Backbone', *Financial Times*, 24 June, p. 18.

Calhoun, C. (2000) 'Resisting Globalisation or Shaping It?', *Prometheus*, 3: 28–47.

Caulkin, S. (2000) 'On their Own and On the Make', *Observer* (Business section), 20 Aug., p. 9.

Curtis, J. (2000) 'All Shook Up', *Financial Times* (The Business, weekend magazine), 12 Feb., pp. 32–5.

Denny, C. (1999a) 'Our Debt to the Web', *Guardian* (Online section), 1 July, pp. 12–13.

Denny, C. (1999b) 'Cyber Utopia? Only the Usual Candidates Need Apply', *Guardian*, 12 July, p. 23.

Denny, C. (2000) 'Poor Countries Face $50bn Bill for Tax Havens', *Guardian*, 24 June, p. 25.

Dillon, J. (2001) 'Doctors to Treat Patients Online', *Independent on Sunday*, 14 Jan., p. 2.

Economist (1996) 'Bangalore Bytes, Software in India', *The Economist*, 23 Mar., p. 85.

Economist (1999a) 'Computers and Wages', *The Economist*, 11 Sept., p. 116.

Economist (1999b) 'Nerd World War: Asia's Lethal Computers', *The Economist*, 30 Oct., p. 88.

Economist (2000a) 'The Future of Work', *The Economist*, 29 Jan., pp. 113–15.

Economist (2000b) 'The Slow Death of Boeing Man', *The Economist*, 18 Mar., pp. 59–60.

Economist (2000c) 'The Human Touch', *The Economist*, 1 July, p. 69.

Economist (2000d) 'Free Music, Free Ride?', *The Economist*, 26 Aug., pp. 92–3.

Economist (2000e) 'Anti-capitalist Protests: Angry and Effective', *The Economist*, 23 Sept., pp. 125–9.

Economist (2000f) 'Come Back!', *The Economist*, 28 Oct., p. 54.

Economist (2001) 'The Internet and the Law', *The Economist*, 13 Jan., pp. 25–7.

Fallows, J. (2000) 'Internet Illusions', *New York Review of Books*, 16 Nov., pp. 28–31.

Financial Times (2001) 'New Economy: Myths and Reality' (editorial), 13 Jan., p. 14.

Gillies, N. (1999) 'When Even the Toilets have Eyes', *Observer* (Business section), 15 Aug., p. 20.

Gillies, N. (2000) 'Bosses Step Up Cyber Snooping', *Observer* (Business section), 4 June, p. 18.

Glaister, D. (1998) 'Britain's Creative Genius Adds up to £50bn Talent a Year', *Guardian*, 7 Nov., p. 26.

Grande, C. (2000) 'Restricted Access to New Technology will Widen Digital Divide', *Financial Times*, 15 July, p. 4.

Halstead, R. (1997) 'Inventor Takes DTI to European Court', *Independent on Sunday* (Business section), 12 Jan., p. 1.

Helmore, E. and McKie, R. (2000) 'Gates Loses Faith in Computers', *Observer*, 5 Nov., p. 5.

Hilpern, K. (2000a) 'How to Keep the Day-Job', *Independent on Sunday* (Smart Moves section), 23 Jan., p. 1.

Hilpern, K. (2000b) 'The Hacked-Off Hackers', *Independent on Sunday* (Business section), 10 Dec., p. 8.

Hirst, C. (2000) 'Hail Ireland, the New California', *Independent on Sunday* (Business section), 30 Apr., p. 4.

Hobsbawm, A. (2000) 'Desktop Lawyers', *Financial Times* (The Business, weekend magazine), 9 Sept., p. 14.

Hutton, W. (1998) 'Thatcher is Not to Blame for Income Inequality: It Could All be Down to Lightweight Fridges and Paperless Dogwalkers', *Observer*, 29 Mar., p. 28.

Inman, P. (2000) 'When a Cheap Shot can Cost you Dear', *Guardian* (Jobs and Money section), 25 Nov., p. 3.

Islam, F. (2000) 'What's Left?', *Observer* (Business section), 17 Dec., p. 5.

Kohn, M. (1999) 'A Virtually Useless Protest', *Independent on Sunday* (Review section), 4 Apr., p. 38.

Lawson, B. (2000) 'Internet, e-mail Opening Job Doors for the Deaf', *Hamilton Spectator*, distributed CSS Internet News, at www.bestnet.org/~jwalker/inews.htm (8 July 2000).

Lewis, L. (2001) 'Killer Bug Hits "Illegal" TV Viewers', *Independent on Sunday* (Business section), 4 Feb., p. 3.

MacErlean, N. (1999) 'Making Homework Less of a Chore', *Observer* (Business section), 16 May, p. 18.

Martinson, J. (2000) 'Gates Derides Digital Donors', *Guardian*, 4 Nov., p. 25.

Moores, S. (2000) 'Upping the Revolution', *Observer* (Business section), 17 Dec., p. 8.

Morgan, O. (2000) 'Official Figures Hide Manufacturing Jobs', *Observer* (Business section), 22 Oct., p. 1.

Motley Fool (2001) 'Fact: The New Economy Does Not Exist', *Independent on Sunday* (Business section), 7 Jan., p. 9.

Naughton, J. (1999) 'How Mean is my Valley', *Observer* (Review section), 4 July, p. 13.

Naughton, J. (2000a) 'Hacked Off by the Insecurities of Cyberspace Gold-Diggers', *Observer* (Business section), 20 Feb., p. 8.

Naughton, J. (2000b) 'Global Net Soars above Legal Eagles', *Observer* (Business section), 28 May, p. 6.

Naughton, J. (2000c) 'Your Privacy Ends Here', *Observer*, 4 June, p. 19.

Naughton, J. (2001) 'Sting in the e-tail will Worry Online Profiteers', *Observer* (Business section), 7 Jan., p. 8.

Oswald, A. (2000) 'Black Gold will Mean Bleak Days', *Observer* (Business Section), 3 Sept., p. 5.

Reeves, R. (2000a) 'All Change in the Workplace: The New Labour Market', *Observer*, 30 Jan., p. 18.

Reeves, R. (2000b) 'No More Nine to Five: The Work Report', *Observer Magazine*, 23 July, pp. 20–7.

Reuters (2000) 'India to Produce More Techies', 1 Nov., available at www.wired.com/news/business/0,1367,39902,00.html (7 Nov. 2000).

184   References

Sardar, Z. (1999) 'The Future is Ours to Change', *New Statesman*, 19 Mar., pp. 25–7.

Schmit, J. and Wiseman, P. (2000) 'Surfing the Dragon', *USA Today* (Money section), 15 Mar., pp. 1–2.

Shaw, W. (2000) 'Cybertopia', *Independent on Sunday* (Review section), 9 July, pp. 10–16.

Summerskill, B. (2000) 'Fluff Mars Rise of Cyberwoman', *Observer*, 27 Aug., p. 17.

Sweet, M. (2000) 'Into the Silicon Valley of Death', *Independent on Sunday* (Review section), 29 Oct., pp. 40–2.

Trapp, R. (2000) 'M'learned, Cut-Price Friends', *Independent on Sunday* (Busness section), 9 July, p. 7.

Vulliamy, E. (2000) 'Slaves Revolt in the Valley of the Dotcoms', *Observer*, 18 June, p. 26.

Walsh, N. P. (2000) 'Mom, I Blew Up the Music Industry', *Observer* (Review section), 21 May, p. 5.

Waters, R. and Grimes, C. (2000) 'Hard Times for the e-book', *Financial Times*, 2 Dec., p. 15.

Index